Tibetan Refugees in India

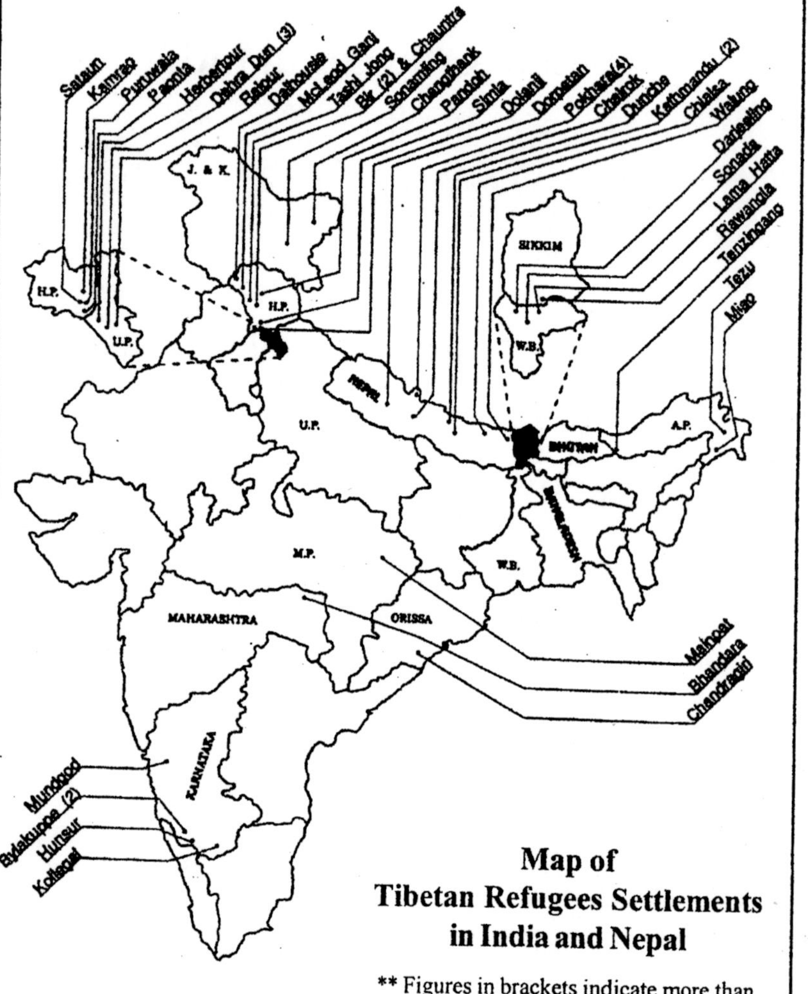

Map of Tibetan Refugees Settlements in India and Nepal

** Figures in brackets indicate more than one settlement in that area.

Tibetan Refugees in India

Rajesh S. Kharat

Kaveri Books
New Delhi - 110 002

Title: Tibetan Refugees in India

First Published in 2003
Edition 2023

ISBN-10: 81-7479-062-4
ISBN-13: 978-81-7479-062-0

Published by
Kaveri Books
4832/24, Ansari Road
New Delhi-110002 (India)
Tel: 011- 4707 2321
E-mail : info@kaveribooks.com
kaveribooks@gmail.com
website: www.kaveribooks.com

Laser Typesetting by
Aarati Computers, Delhi - 110 009

PRINTED IN INDIA

Dedicated
To

Apa B. Pant

Preface

It is a well known fact that the problem of Tibetan refugees is a living problem and it is bound to remain so for many years to come. In fact it is very much true that despite constant protests made by Communist China on the issue of Tibetan refugees, the Government of India remains in a state of readiness to tackle the problem on a scale and in a manner which the magnitude and intensity of the problem demand. The grant of asylum to political and religious refugees has been the tradition of every civilized community and it will be a humiliating degeneration of our political practice if these unfortunate, helpless and destitute victims were denied the privilege of being sheltered under the roof of India.

Repatriation is not the ultimate, real solution of the problem of Tibetan refugees. On the contrary the immediate problems and important questions of these refugees are the three basic needs of livelihood, food, clothing and shelter. Besides this, medical aid education, employment, settlement and finally absorption come to the forefront. These questions are not temporary or time being concerns at least in the case of Tibetan refugees. So, one has to foresee the long-term time solutions in terms of future generation of Tibetan refugees.

Every one knows that at the request of the Dalai Lama, the Government of India granted asylum to him and his followers purely on humanitarian grounds and also undertook some long-term rehabilitation schemes for them. But unfortunately due to the various circumstances and conditions it had a wider impact on the local people in the vicinity areas of Tibetan refugee camps in India, particularly in the northern and north-eastern states of India. This is how the situation of Tibetan refugees in India provoked me to undertake this study and make an attempt to find out the action/reaction of the local people vis-à-vis Tibetans in and around the settlement camps.

Along with brief discussion in the first chapter on the concepts like 'Refugee', 'IDPs' 'Asylum seekers', 'Economic Migrants' and 'Citizenship' in an Introduction, the major part of this study deals with the *Historical Background of Tibetan Refugees* within China in its chapter two. The third chapter, Survival in Exile makes an attempt to find out how the Government of India managed to assist and rehabilitate the mass influx of Tibetan refugees with available resources and remedies. Emphasis is placed on the various rehabilitation programmes and development assistance provided by the Government of India along with numerous international and domestic agencies and aid donor countries. This chapter also surveys the grievances of Tibetan refugees who are scattered all over India and yet not rehabilitated in the settlement camps either by the Government of India or the Central Tibetan Administration. The fourth chapter *Reconstruction of Tibet in Exile* investigates whether the Tibetan Refugees were successful in preserving and protecting their unique culture of Tibetan art and traditions while in refuge in India. The chapter five *Implications on India as a Host Nation* has been discussed on the basis of my personal observations and detailed interviews with local people, Tibetan office bearers in Dharamsala and fresh arrivals of Tibetans in scattered camps and Rehabilitation Camps Himachal Pradesh. Lastly, in the conclusion, The study also makes an attempt to find out the status of various other refugees from different part of the sub-continent in general and India's immediate reactions of the Tibetan refugees in particular. Especially does the response from local people matter a lot when it comes to the practical aspects of socio-economic adaptation, the areas of these settlement camps and thereby the evaluation of the careful handling of the issue of Tibetan refugees.

To complete this study I have received a Travel Grant of Rs.10,000 from the Department's Special Assistance (DSA) Programme, the Scheme of University Grants Commission (UGC) awarded to Department of Civics & Politics, University of Mumbai. The Field Trip to Tibetan Refugee Camps in Himachal Pradesh was conducted during May- June 1999.

I have the most pleasant obligation to thank the Dalai Lama for his immediate response and letter to my request for allowing me to conduct field trip to Tibetan Refugee Camps in India. I also thank Dr. Aditi Pant, Director, NCL at Pune and daughter of Apa B.Pant (India's Political Officer to Sikkim, Bhutan and Tibet) for sharing her thoughts and views on H.H. The Dalai Lama. In preparing this study I have received numerous suggestions from Rajen Harshe, Professor at Department of Political Science, University of Hyderabad and Prof. Dawa Norbu, my teacher from School of International Studies, JNU, New Delhi, Thubten Samphel, Secretary to Ministry of Foreign Affairs, Tibetan Government in Exile, A.C. Sinha and Tanka B. Subba, Professors at Department of Social Anthropology, NEHU, Shillong. My special thanks to them for their constant guidance in this work.

I am also thankful to Bhalchandra Mungekar, Vice-Chancellor, University of Mumbai and Chairman, DSA Advisory Committee as well as Prof. Nawaz B. Mody, Coordinator of the DSA Programme and Professor and Head, Department of Civics & Politics, University of Mumahi, for their constant pressure and support to complete this study.

I must record my sincere thanks and gratefulness to all who encouraged me in pursuance of this study especially, S. D. Muni, my teacher, Ex-Indian Ambassador to Laos and Professor at School of International Studies, JNU, New Delhi, Lionel Fernandes, Former Head, Department of Civics & Politics, University of Mumbai, Sharit Bhowmik, Professor at Department of Sociology, University of Mumbai, who gave me an opportunity to interact many scholars on Tibet and refugees at Centre of Himalayan Studies, NBU, Darjeeling. Om Prakash Misra, Director, Centre for Refugee Studies, at Jadavpur University, Kolkata who invited me to present paper on Tibetan refugees at International Seminar on Forced Migration in South Asia, to clarify my doubts about this Project. In the same manner Mohan Prabhu, Dy. Director ICSSR(WRC) Mumbai, and I.N. Mukherji, my teacher and Dean, School of International Studies, JNU, New Delhi who also made it possible for me to attend and present a paper on Tibetan refugees at International Conference on Global Refugees at British Sociological Association, Stafford University, UK.

I am also grateful to my colleagues from the University of Mumbai, in particular, I owe my thanks to M. Muralidhara, Department of Civics & Politics, my friend Arun Kamble, Head, Department of Marathi. T.R. Ghoble, Reader in History, University of Mumbai deserves special thanks for enlightening me on Tibetan Buddhism.

I must acknowledge the facilities which I have used during the course of my research work, which were offered to me by the staff of the Library of Tibetan Work and Archives, McLeod Ganj, H.P. and Library of University of Mumbai.

Responsibility for the criticisms made and views are expressed in the book rests solely with me.

8 March 2003 **Rajesh S Kharat**
Mumbai

Contents

1

AN INTRODUCTION TO THE TERM *REFUGEE*

The post World War period has witnessed a large number of political upheavals in many countries. The European and Third World countries are the most affected. Millions are being forced to leave their homeland due to the various policies and actions by governments and sometimes also due to the inability of governments to protect the weaker sections of the society. Reasons for such disturbances range from simple political rivalry, regional conflicts of a country, ethnic issues, socio-economic tensions, unequal distribution of natural resources and development projects to simple persecution of minorities of one country by another, or, of one region by another region due to racial discrimination.

All these create refugees, internally displaced persons (IDPs), asylum seekers, migrants and immigrants. In the case of refugees as well as IDPs, the situation is not very happy because of fear of international repercussions. Most of the regimes in the Third World and developed countries do not recognize the existence of refugees or IDPs. The refugees, themselves become uprooted people with very little or no state protection and continue to face the hostility of the local people wherever they are forced to stay. The Indian sub-continent is known for the largest movement of refugees since the post World War II period. Almost each and every country in the South Asian region is facing the problem of refugees generated by them, except India. For instance, Rohingyas in Bangladesh, Bhutanese refugees in Nepal, Tamil refugees in India, Tibetan refugees in Karnataka and the north-eastern parts of India and Chakmas in the states of Tripura and Arunachal Pradesh. In general, refugees are forced migrants living without national boundaries and government protection. Most of them want to flee as far as possible from the conflict but they are not welcome. However, most of the time, once they have crossed over illegally into other country, they live without any formal documentation and identity cards. This results in problems of economic opportunities, social-cultural and ethnic conflicts between the host population and the refugees. Moreover, it leads to increasing hostility between the refugee generating countries and the host nations, thereby worsening traditional cordial relationships with each other. For example, Sino-India relations on the issue of Tibetan refugees, Indo–Bangladesh relations on the issue of Chakma refugees, Indo-Sri Lanka over the issue of Tamil refugees, Bhutan–Nepal relations on the issue of Bhutanese refugees are examples. Once the issue of refugees is highlighted at international platforms and gatherings, naturally under the pressure of the world public opinion or many diplomatic initiatives the refugee generating countries are bound to mellow down their harsh treatment to its weaker section or minorities. Many times this interference or humanitarian intervention by a third country or organization has been viewed as a threat to its sovereignty, territorial integrity and independent status of the affected country. Thus in the contemporary world, the refugees have become the major concern and subject of not only one nation but also of overall international relations.

Definition of Refugee within the Mandate of UNHCR

It has been observed that most of the time, genuine refugees are not recognized due to the technical difficulties, as they do not fall into the category of formal definition of refugees. So they are deprived from not only the international coverage but also from international aid and sympathy. In this context it is important that one should take note of the definition of *refugee* in general and the definition used by the United Nations in particular, and how these are distinct from the internally displaced persons (IDPS), stateless persons, asylum seekers, economic migrants, and citizens.

The 1951Convention Relating the Status of Refugees

After World War II, for the first time, the UN made an attempt to define the term *refugee* as most of the European countries had suffered due to a refugee crisis. The most widely accepted definition of *refugee* is that contained in the 1951 Convention. It defines *refugee* in Article 1A (2) as,

> Any person who as a result of events occurring before 1 January 1951 and owing to well-founded fear of being persecuted for reasons of race, religion, nationality, membership of a particular social group or political opinion, is outside the country of his nationality and is unable or, owing to such fear, is unwilling to avail himself of the protection of that country; or who, not having a nationality and being outside the country of his former habitual residence as a result of such-events, is unable or, owing to such fear, is unwilling to return to it.

Since the above definition viewed as it requires that a person be outside his or her country, it effectively excludes the internally displaced persons from receiving international protection. In addition to this it focuses on individualized persecution. Thus it does not recognize a situation of generalized violence such as natural disasters, or large scale development projects as legitimate reasons for flight. Moreover the 1951 Convention was looked upon as Eurocentric, and does not define and demarcate the line for the status of refugees in other parts of the world. So the term *refugee* was defined in a wider manner through the 1967 Protocol and two other Regional Instruments known as:

1. *1969 Organization for African Unity (OAU) Convention Governing the Specific Aspects of Refugee Problems in Africa.*
2. *1984 Cartagena Declaration on Refugees.*

The 1967 Protocol

The important feature of the Protocol of 31 January 1967 relating to the Status of Refugees (hereafter the 1967 Protocol) was that it removed the temporal and geographical limitations contained in the 1951 Convention. Despite this, there was an argument from various corners that efforts were not made by the UN to reconsider the definition of the term *refugee*. "This meant that most third world refugees continued to remain *de facto* excluded, as their flight has been frequently prompted by natural disaster, war, or political and economic turmoil rather than by persecution, at least as that term is understood in the Western context."[1] Thus at the regional level different definitions of *refugee* have been adopted, namely, the *OAU Convention* and the *Cartagena Declaration* which examines the conditions under which the different definitions were adopted in Africa and Latin America and their salient features.

The OAU Convention of 1969

The first broader definition of *refugee* was advanced in the 1969 OAU Convention. Article 1 of the *OAU Convention* definition incorporated the earlier definitions and added:

> The term 'refugee' shall also apply to every person who, owing to external aggression, occupation, foreign domination or events seriously disturbing public order in either part or the whole of his country of origin or nationality, is compelled to leave his place of habitual residence in order to seek refugee in another place outside his country of origin or nationality.

This was the first time that at the regional level, the definition was extended to individuals forced to leave their countries owing to aggression by another State or as a result of an invasion. *The OAU Convention* is treated as a benchmark for the beginning of a refugee protection system.

The 1984 Cartagena Declaration

It was this 1984 Colloquium that resulted in the most encompassing definition of refugee for Latin America to date. *The 1984 Cartagena Declaration* calls for :

> consideration of the objective situation in the country of origin and the particular situation of the person or groups of persons seeking protection as refugees. This definition requires that two conditions be met to be declared a refugee: that there exist a threat to life, security, or liberty; and that the threat result from one of five factors: generalized violence; foreign aggression; international conflicts; massive violations of human rights; or circumstances seriously disturbing public order.

A total of 139 countries have signed the 1951 Geneva Refugee Convention and/or its 1967 Protocol and recognize persons as refugees based on the definitions contained in these and the regional instruments.

The 1966 Bangkok Principles

In *Article 1 of the 1966 Principles concerning Treatment of Refugees adopted by the Asian –African Legal Consultative Committee*, the term *refugee* which applies mostly as per the situation in the Asian Countries is defined as,

> A refugee is a person who, owing to persecution or well-founded fear of persecution for reasons of race, colour, religion, political belief or membership of a particular social group:
>
> (a) leaves the State of which he is a national, or the Country of his nationality, or, if he has no nationality, the State or Country of which he is a habitual resident; or
>
> (b) being outside such State or Country, is unable or unwilling to return to it or to avail himself of its protection.
>
> Two Exceptions attached to this Article states:
>
> (1) A person having more than one nationality shall not be a refugee if he is in a position to avail himself of the protection of any State or Country of which he is a national.
>
> (2) A person who prior to his admission into the Country of refugee, has committed a crime against peace, a war crime, or a crime against humanity or a serious non-political crime or has committed acts contrary to the purposes and principles of the United Nations shall not be refugee.

Stateless Persons

In general terms an alien may, as we have seen, be one without any nationality that is a stateless person. Although one can argue on the legal position of a stateless person as compared with aliens possessing nationality but in practice stateless persons are in most states treated more or less as though they were subjects or citizens of a foreign state. The fact is that the stateless person is without nationality and does not enjoy the protection of his country of origin. His national status is uncertain.

To distinguish *refugees* from the *stateless persons*, one must observe the difference between *The 1951 Convention* which addresses the problem of *refugees*, and the *Convention Relating to the Status of Stateless Persons, 1954* which makes general provision like non-discrimination as between stateless persons on the ground of race, religion or country of origin (Article 3) exemption from reciprocity (Article 7), which came into force in 1960. It defines a *stateless person* as a 'person who is not considered as a national by any State under the operation of its law'.[2]

For instance, certain groups of war-affected populations, are *stateless* citizens of the former Soviet Union who have not been able to obtain the nationality of any of the new countries which emerged after the dissolution of the USSR like Uzbekistan.

Internally Displaced Persons (IDPs)

There is no unanimity among scholars about the definition of IDPs. Every scholar or an institution has its own way of perception of the definition of IDPs, and accordingly, the concept of IDPs has been discussed along the following lines.

According to Janie Hampton, Editor of *Internally Displaced People: A Global Survey:*

> Unlike refugees who cross international borders, those who stay within their own country must rely upon their own

> governments to uphold their civil and human rights. If the state chooses not to invite external assistance, then the international community has limited options to protect these people. In many countries it is the government or its military forces that have caused the displacement or prevented access to their citizens.[3]

The definition for internally displaced people (IDPs) used by the United Nations:

> Persons or groups of persons who have been forced to flee or to leave their homes or places of habitual residence as a result of, or in order to avoid, in particular, the effects of armed conflict, situations of generalized violence, violations of human rights or natural or human-made disasters, and who have not crossed an internationally recognized state border.[4]

Although it is a very vague definition, it attempts to include all aspects of internal displacement. It assumes that the international aid community will become concerned, particularly where violations of human rights occur. Ironically, in practice, as per *IDP: Global Survey (1997)*, sometimes the governments concerned, exaggerate a problem in order to secure more international aid.

Thus it is very difficult to define those who are IDPs, because people are forced to flee from their homes because of either civil or international war (Afghanistan, Sri Lanka, Israel, Palestine, Iran, Iraq and Africa as well as in Eastern Europe); natural or man-made disasters, (China Japan, Korea, Australia and some of the South-East Asian Countries); development like construction of dams or urban clearances (India, Bangladesh) and changes in the economy due to either industrialization or famine (Philippines, Malaysia, Cambodia, Thailand, Hong Kong, Taiwan, and Fiji). Although there are certain cases of economic migrations for example, the continuous flow of Bengali Muslims from Bangladesh to India and the flow of Asian people in the United Kingdom or the United States of America would be good examples of this kind. However one cannot go on arguing the various reasons for internal displacement within one nation, and from one nation to another for the sake of economic, cultural and social security. They include, and an estimated 5.4 million internally displaced persons. The IDPs are the fastest growing group of displaced persons in the world. Because they, in effect, 'fall between the cracks' of current humanitarian law and assistance, a widespread international debate has been launched on how best to help all IDPs and who should be responsible for their well-being.

Asylum Seekers

> When people flee their own country and seek sanctuary in a second state, they apply for 'asylum' – or the right to be recognized as bona fide refugees and the legal protection and material assistance that status implies.[5]

The Post World War II world witnessed several million people who were granted asylum in countries around the world. Some refugees cannot or are unwilling to return home, usually because they would face continued persecution. For in West Asia most of the Iraqis and Iranis did not go back to their homes even after the end of the Iran – Iraq war due to fear of punishment. The samething applies to Palestine refugees, Sudanese refugees, Chakma refugees and Tibetan refugees. In such circumstances, the UNHCR helps to find them new homes, either in the asylum country where they are living, or in third countries where they can be permanently resettled.

Refugees have a fundamental right to safe asylum. This right – to seek and enjoy refuge from persecution or war – is enshrined in the Universal Declaration of Human Rights of 1948 and is a basic principle of international law. It is an ancient and widely respected practice of civilized states, and an international obligation. Therefore many nations have agreed to accept refugees on a temporary basis during the early phases of a crisis, only around a dozen countries have regular resettlement programmes and accept quotas of refugees on an annual basis. For example, Britain is treated as a heaven for asylum seekers in Europe, whereas in South Asia, India has become a heaven for the asylum seekers not only for asylum seekers and refugees, but also for terrorists from various parts of the world.

Economic Migrants

B.S. Chimni in his book *International Refugee Law: A Reader* (2000) mentioned:

> A migrant is a person who, for reason other than those contained in the definition, voluntarily leaves his country in order to take up residence elsewhere. He may be moved by the desire for change or adventure, or by family or other reasons of a personal nature. If he is moved exclusively by economic considerations, he is an economic migrant and not a refugee.[6]

The best example of this kind would be Bangladeshi people who had come to India during the pre-1971 and post 1971 periods. Most of them crossed the borders in search of a livelihood and better economic opportunities. Mumbai and Calcutta are the most affected metros of India due to these Bangladesh economic migrants. This is the reason why UNHCR India office does not recognize them as refugees.

Citizenship

One cannot complete the understanding of the above concepts namely, refugees, stateless persons, internally displaced persons, asylum seekers and economic migrants unless and until the meaning of citizenship is spelled out in legal terms.

The term *citizen* is ordinarily used to denote the relation an individual bears to his state or sovereign. The derivation of the word *citizen* from the Latin *civitas* conveys the idea of connection or identification with the state or government and participation in its functions. The term *citizen* emphasizes the rights and privileges as it were, of the status, rather than its correlative obligations. Rousseau drew a distinction between the *subjects* as the passive and the *citizen* as the active member of the political community. However in the contemporary world of the twenty first century no one follows this distinction. To quote A.N. Sinha:

> A citizen then is one who by reason of his birth, naturalization or otherwise is a member of an independent political society, called a state, kingdom, or empire. He is subject to its laws and entitle to its protection in all his rights incidental to that relation.[7]

With special reference to India and being a non-signatory to *The 1951 Convention of the Status of Refugees*, one should look into the details of Citizenship Act provided in the Constitution of India.

Citizenship of India After the Commencement of the Constitution

The Citizenship Act of 1955 (No.57 of 1955) embodies the law of Indian citizenship of persons born on or after 26 January 1950. It supplements the provisions of the Constitution of India and is the permanent law of citizenship of the country. The Act consists of only nineteen sections and three schedules. It provides for acquisition and termination of Indian citizenship. Other provisions are supplemental and they include recognition of Commonwealth citizenship in India.

Acquisition of citizenship may be involuntary or voluntary. Citizenship may be acquired in India by five methods. These are:

1. By birth in India
2. By descent,
3. By registration,
4. By naturalization, and
5. By incorporation of territory.

The acquisition of citizenship by birth and descent and the termination of citizenship on the voluntary acquisition of citizenship of another country have been made retrospective with effect from 26 January 1950. This is to provide for the gap between that date and the date of enactment of the Citizenship Act, 1955, which came into operation from 30 December 1955.

Citizenship by Birth

Every person born in India on or after 26 January 1950, with two exceptions, viz. the children of a person not a citizen of

India and enjoying diplomatic immunity and the children of an enemy alien born in a place which at the time of the child's birth is under enemy occupation, is a citizen of India. This provision of the Citizenship Act, 1955 recognizes and gives effect, as complete as it can be, to the principle of *jus soli*. The mere fact of birth is decisive of citizenship. The nationality of the parents of a child is irrelevant and so is its legitimacy.[8]

In the light of all this, the proposed study makes an attempt to study the presence of Tibetan Refugees in India and its implications.

References

1. B.S. Chimni,(Ed.); *International Refugee Law: A Reader*, (New Delhi: Sage 2001) pp.7-8
2. Ibid. p.9
3. Hampton, Janie, (Ed.); *Internally Displaced People: A Global Survey*, (London: Earth scan Pub. Ltd. 1997) p. xvi
4. Ibid.
5. *Refugees by Numbers 2000 Edition*, (Geneva: UNHCR Publication, 2000), p.10
6. B.S. Chimni, no.1, p.55
7. A.N. Sinha, *Law of Citizenship and Aliens in India*, (Bombay: Asia Publishing House, 1962) pp.4-5
8. For details see Appendix VIII.

2

Historical Background of Tibetan Refugees

Tibet – the Land

Geographically, the Tibetan highland, including the three provinces of Tibet – Amdo, Kham and U-Tsang, extends over and area of 600,000 sq. miles (2.5 million sq. kilometres), more than two-thirds the size of India and is composed of a plateau averaging some 11,000 ft. (3,650 metres) above sea level, lies between 27⁰ C and 37⁰ C North latitude. This high altitude and fairly high latitude conspire to make it one of the coldest countries in the world. Tibet is surrounded by the Himalayas, the Karakorum, Kunlun and Altya-tagh mountain ranges. The area stretches almost 1.5 thousand miles (2500 kms) from west to east and is the source of many great rivers such as the Yangtse, Mekong, Brahmaputra, Salween, Indus, Sutlej, Kali Gandaki, Trisuli, Manas and Subansiri. However the average rainfall is not more than twenty centimetres, the soil is frozen for nearly eight months in the year and during the other four it is dusty. There are rich forests and woods with a lot of useful timber such as birch, poplar, oak, conifers, and buckwheat and in some valleys, rice is also cultivated. Apart from barren land, the remote and relative isolation of this region resulted in a mainly pastoral and nomadic economy in the east and north. But a more settled and broadly-based farming economy in the river valleys and the warmer southern regions.

The geographic, ethnic and political boundaries during the pre-1950 period were very complex. It borders on the erstwhile Soviet Union, India, Myanmar, Bhutan, Nepal and China. The ethnic boundaries of Tibet however, stretch beyond the political. Population of the Tibet race inhabit Nepal, especially in Tamang region, Bhutan Sikkim and along the westward Himalayas they are found in varying numbers in the Indian hill districts of Garhwal, Kullu, Spiti, Lahaul, Ladakh, Kashmir and NEFA (Arunachal Pradesh).[1] This shows there were many Tibetans who had settled in India much before the post – 1959 event, living peacefully, while maintaining cordial relations with the local inhabitants of India.

The question of a political boundary is undoubtedly the most controversial. In 1914, the British negotiated an agreement with the Dalai Lama, the result of which was the division of Tibet into Inner and Outer Tibet. In the course of history Russia always claimed control over portions of Tibet lying across her own borders. The Chinese claim that Tibet is an integral part of the Chinese Republic, which led to the present crisis of Tibet and Tibetans. This has happened according to Chanakya Sen because factually, the Tibetan administration in Lhasa has never been able to extend its effective control to more than half of geographical Tibet.[2]

Amauny de Reincort, author of *Lost World – Tibet, Key to Asia*, who was then in Lhasa, a scholar who described first time and realized the strategic significance of Tibet in the world during the period of World War II. He mentioned in his book:

> I was struck by the strategic potentialities of the Roof of the World, of this Colossal natural fortress standing in the heart of Asia and almost inaccessible by land. Behind the Cyclopean Himalayas and Kuen Lun mountain ranges, Tibet towers an

> all sides above the three most populated countries in the world: China five hundred million, India is four hundred and the USSR's two hundred. Any strong power based on the Chang Tang would control the heart of Asia – not only would such bases are but an hour's flight from India's Delhi and two or three hours from China's Chunking. ..... I became convinced that if even Tibet was taken over by the Soviets or the Chinese communists, the whole of India and of South – East Asia would become strategically untenable and left wide open to an invasion.[3]

As far as India is concerned, Tibet has a great strategic significance to India. The high altitude of Tibet and its geographical location has been a most effective natural barrier against the possible Chinese aggressive designs in the Himalayas. Thus Tibet has direct links with India's security interest in the north.

Religion, Culture and People

The majority of Tibetans profess Mahayana Buddhism and are followers of Lamaism. For them, religion and traditions form the essential basis of life which is regulated by "Divine Will" whose interpreters are Lamas. Before the advent of Buddhism the religion prevailing in Tibet was Bon-Po[4] which had abundant traces of Indian and Chinese influences. Buddhism came to Tibet from both India and China. Buddhism had to fight a grim battle with Bon-Po resulting ultimately in Lamaism, a mixture of both.[5] Nevertheless, Tibet is best known for its Buddhism. "In Tibet, there are four sects, all somewhat different in their methods and political persuasions but not in their reverence for and allegiance to the basic Buddhist doctrines".[6] These four sects are often distinguished by the colour of the headdresses worn for ceremonial occasions, are known as Nyingmpa, Korgyu, Sakya and Gelugpa. All enjoyed varying periods of pre-dominance in Tibet; but it was the Gelugpa, or Yellow Hat Sect, that maintained absolute political power from the eighteenth century until 1959. Almost all Tibetans except a very small number of practitioners of an earlier religion known as Bon and a handful of Muslims consider themselves Buddhists.

But Tibetan Buddhism has a strong belief in the supernatural because it is "heavily influenced by the environmental realities of living in such a harsh land; the severe cold and winds the effects of the rarefied air, the almost complete isolation from the rest of the world, and the resulting lack of scientific knowledge".[8]

In the field of culture, India's influence was more pronounced. The first great Tibetan King *Son-Tsan-Gom-Po* in the early seventh century sent a great statesman to India to study and work out an alphabet for the Tibetan languages. On his return to Lhasa this statesman, whose name was *Tho-Mi-Sam-Bho-Ta* and his sixteen companions invented a Tibetan alphabet, which was based on the Brahmi character then in vogue in Kashmir.[9] Moreover, Tibetan art is to a large extent a continuation of the medieval Buddhist art of Bihar and Orissa. Paintings and sculptures are almost totally influenced by Indian traditions. In addition to this, the Tibetan recites and chants his *mantra* or prayer which starts from Om, (Om Mani Padme Om), signifying the Indian influence on Tibetan culture. As Buddhism migrated to Tibet from India, India may be called the spiritual home of Tibetans.

The origins of the Tibetan people remain obscure. The Tibetans may be the descendents of the nomadic non-Chinese Chiang tribes of East Central Asia or possibly of earlier Ural-Altaic people.[9] Tibetan society was originally nomadic in nature and gradually evolved into a system where the land belong to the state but was held in estates by the government, monasteries or aristocracy. Tenant farmers worked in the land, many of them bound to the estate, but to none of the various kinds of relationships whereby tenants paid taxes to their landlords do the terms *Serfdom* or *Slavery* seem to apply.[10] The other life-styles existed nomadic, merchants, semi-nomadic peasants and craftsmen. In the provinces of *Kham* and *Amdo* (E.Tibet) where fewer big estates existed and there were larger free peasant's holdings, more individuals owned their land and paid taxes directly to the government.

Political System

Politically, Tibetans were ruled by an unusual form of feudal theocracy that was both centralized and decentralized. A centralized government in Lhasa was headed by a man known as the Dalai Lama, who was at the very top of the social and political structure and both the secular and ecclesiastical ruler of Tibet.[11] The central government maintained a military force, issued currency and postage stamps, negotiated with other governments and acted as a final court of appeal. Whereas, the decentralized government gives local control to the countless monastic and aristocratic estates, who essentially came from noble families.[12] The noble's main function as government officials as quite straightforward; to collect taxes, settle disputes, punish criminals, and act as liaison between the Central government and the area of Tibet they were administering.[13] Since the values in Tibetan society are combined with religion and politics, the institution of the Dalai Lama is regarded not only as spiritual leader but also political head of Tibet. Tibetans believe that he is the incarnation of the patron deity of Tibet, *Chenrezig* (known in India Buddhism as Analoketisvara).

Thus, to describe the patter of the Tibetan Government during pre – 1950 Tibet, after Dalai Lama at the top, it consisted then of the Chief Minister, and then the cabinet of one priest and three laymen. Next came the ecclesiastical court which dealt with matters concerning the large body of monks in the country, and below this the National Assembly or Parliament. The cabinet was known as the *Kashag* and each cabinet member is known as a *Shape*. The *Kashag* has a general controlling power over the internal administration of the country, whether in political, revenue or *Tsong-du*, the Tibetan equivalent of parliament is composed of all secular and ecclesiastical officials below the members of *Kashag*. The total number of officials in Tibet is usually around three hundred and fifty, half of them lay and half ecclesiastical.[14]

According to Patterson, "Decisions are not put to the vote, but from the way that the discussion goes the minority opinion will gradually drop out and the conclusion be arrived at by those who hold the floor."[15] However for all practical purposes, the Dalai Lama was the sole decision-maker, all decisions from being communicated and reported to him. The influence of the institution of Dalai Lama is rightly expressed in a Tibetan proverb: "If he tells you to strike a rock, strike! If he tells you to go to hell, Go!"[16]

Pre-1914 Tibet

The first definite contacts between the two peoples were in the Tang dynasty (AD618 – 907), when about a hundred missions passed between the two countries. These were either simply goodwill missions carrying gifts and compliments, or diplomatic parties making treaties or renewing friendly relation.[17]

In the seventh century Tibet's most famous king, *Srongtsen Gampo*, extended Tibet's power right into China and Nepal and had a huge empire, extended north into Chinese Turkistan, westwards into Central Asia and even into China itself. During this period, the Tibetans captured the then Chinese province Shensi and on the flight of the emperor, appointed a new emperor of their own.[18] It was at this period that Buddhism was introduced into Tibet by the Chinese and Nepali wives of Srongtsen Gompo and then in the reign of Tihtsong Detsen (AD 741) by pundits from India. Towards the end of the ninth century there was a religious revival throughout Tibet and a treaty was signed with Chine in AD 877 dealing with the boundaries then fixed between Tibet and China at *Chorten Karpo*.[19] Thus, between the seventh and ninth centuries, Tibet as a military power was by no means inferior to China. But later, when it was divided and weakened, its foreign relations were reduced almost to naught and resulted in collapse of Tibetan empire by the end of the tenth century. For the next three hundred years Tibet's relations either with China or any other country remained minimal.

In the thirteenth century Tibet became a vassal state of the all conquering moguls under Jenghis Khan. During this time, the nephew of the famous *Sakya Pandita* of the large *Sakya* monastery; *Phagspa* visited Kublai Khan in 1253, he became so popular that he was made *Kubali's* spiritual guide. Subsequently he was raised to the rank of priest – king of Tibet and constituted the ruler of: (1) Tibet proper, comprising the thirteen districts of *U - Tsang* (2) *Kham* and (3) *Amdo*.[20]

During this period, corrupt practices, like, devil worshipping, and constant inter-monastery fighting of the Lamas or priests, resulted in the Buddhist religion being in danger of becoming extinct. In the middle of the fourteenth century the great religious reformer *Tsong-Ka-Pa*, was born and revived the religion in a purer form, curtailed all ill practices and superstitions worship. He founded a sect known as *Gelugpa* (those who follow the path of perfect visiting and in 1409 established his first monastery called *Gaden* (Place of joy), and subsequently other two, namely, *Drepung* (1416) and *Sera*(1419). All three of these monasteries were in the Lhasa area and were to become pre-eminent in the ruling of Tibet. The *Gelugpa* became known as the *Yellow Hat* sect.[21] While others were commonly grouped under *Red Hats* – names that derived from the colours of hats worn during ceremonial function. According to Tibetan history, till the emergence of the fifth Dalai Lama, the Dalai Lama was the undisputed leader of only one and not the most powerful sect, the *Gelugpas*. He held no temporal power. However, the fifth Dalai Lama's close alliance with the Mogol military, gave him the best opportunity to win that power. The Mongolian chief after invading Tibet handed over the sovereignty of the whole of Tibet to the fifth Dalai Lama in 1641.[22] Thus, for the first time, under him, the spiritual and secular authority of the Dalai Lama was established, and since then it is still maintained by the Dalai Lama.

It is safe to say that, Tibet's relations with China were maintained in a true sense during the fifth Dalai Lama, when he was invited to Peking by the Manchurian Empire *Shih-Tsu* in 1652 where he was treated with profound respect and courtesy. This event can be seen as a turning point in the political history of Tibet and its status. Two different views were expressed by the scholars on Tibetan history. According to Charles Bell, "the fifth Dalai Lama, when visiting Peking in AD 1652 came there as an independent monarch, being at that time neither under China nor under any other nation"[23] whereas another reputed scholar, W.W. Rockhill says: "The Dalai Lama had been treated with all the ceremony which could have been accorded to any independent sovereign. Indeed, the emperor treated him well, and took every precaution not to offend him."[24]

On these views, Cammann points out, "reception done is not sufficient evidence that he was considered an independent sovereign."[25] Thus, for a reader it is very difficult to infer any final opinion regarding the status of Tibet. Basically, in the whole medieval history nothing certain, all the political developments, and activities were ruled by the push and pull factor of the power centres. So we cannot conclude that Tibet was an independent or dependent state in history. During that period, the status of a state, especially a small and weak state like Tibet, was primarily determined by various factors such as political, economic self-sufficiency, military power and sovereignty at the internal and external levels, mainly its relations with major states powerful neighbourings state like Bhutan, India or Kuwait, Iraq and so on. Taking into consideration the status of Tibet, which determined by the domestic potentials in China and its strength in the outside world, the Chinese declared Tibet as part of it for own convenience and to suit its national interest. However, to know why Chinese emperor treated the Dalai Lama tactfully with profound respect and courtesy, one can refer to the following the quote from W.W. Rockhill,

> at this period of China's relations with Tibet, the temporal power of the Lama, backed by the arms of Ghusi Khan and the devotion of all moguls was not a thing for the emperor of China to question.[26]

As a result of this Chinese did not declare its claim on Tibet. Therefore there is no solid reason to believe the Chinese claim on Tibet as an integral part of China and there is scope to safely say that Tibet was an independent and sovereign state in the fifteenth century.

After the death of the fifth Dalai Lama, in 1682, his successor the sixth Dalai Lama, too was invited to Peking, but died – some claim he was murdered on the way.[27] In view of his alleged indulgence in wine, women and indecent behaviour, there was a dispute regarding his sincerity and genius as the sixth Dalai Lama, which encouraged the Chinese to set up the seventh Dalai Lama on its own and incarnate him on Tibet's throne. But this attempt of China to control Tibet indirectly was scuttled, when the Mongolian army invaded Tibet and established its regime.

The demoralized Chinese once again made an attempt to invade Tibet in 1720 and followed traditional Chinese war tactics "encirclement and suppression campaign" against its enemies. Through these methods, finally, the Chinese entered Lhasa and installed a new and seventh Dalai Lama. This was the occasion, when the Chinese began claiming their suzerainty over Tibet. After the invasion of Tibet the moguls influence was totally eroded and the vacuum was filled by the 3000 Chinese soldiers who monitored the developments within and outside of Tibet. Chinese demarcated the new boundary line between China and Tibet by erecting a pillar in 1727 at Bum-La.[28] According to this boundary line,

> ...the western part of the Tibet was handed over to the rule of the Dalai Lama under the sovereignty of the Manchu emperor, while Tibetan chiefs of the states and tribes in the provinces of Khan and Amdo to the east of it were given the status of Semi-independent feudatories of China. [29]

This status of Tibet was acknowledged by George Bogle, "The Chinese in general are committed to the capital, no tribute is exacted, ant the people of Tibet, except Lhasa, hardly feel the weight of a foreign yoke."[30]

Later on in 1790, when the Gurkhas of Nepal invaded Tibet, the Chinese army marched into Tibet and defeated them, and advanced its army close to Kathmandu, the capital of Nepal. Thus, Nepal was forced to the sign a humiliating peace treaty with China, agreeing to restore all the plunder taken and to send a tribute mission to Peking every five years.[31]

Realizing the strategic significance of Tibet and adjoining territories, the Manchus decided to consolidate their position and strengthen their hold over their newly- acquired territory on the Indian border. To do so, the Chinese carried out certain programmes in Tibet through the Resident Commissioner. For instance, control of the treasury and the introduction of a new currency, bearing the title of the emperor, reforms in administration, defined the duties and responsibilities of each official. Moreover, all communication with neighbouring states such as Nepal, Bhutan and Sikkim had to be conducted through the Resident and any entry into or departure from Tibetan territory had first to be approved by him.[32] This absolute control of China over Tibet did not remain for long as the Chinese position was weakened because of the Anglo-Chinese War or the Opium war of 1840. In addition to this, the Taiping rebellion deteriorated the Chinese position, China also being defeated by the combined armies of England and France. This led to Chinese disinterest in Tibet for some time.

In 1860, the Tibetans of Nyarong in Khan, east Tibet, under the leadership of Gombu Namgyar, invaded and conquered the neighbouring state and halted any communications between China and Tibet for the next few years. As a result, on request for help, from the neighbouring states, the Tibetan Government in Lhasa as well the Chinese Government suppress the disturbances and killed Gombu Namgyal. Thereafter, it is said that, the responsibility of administration of reacquired states and territory was formally handed over to the Dalai Lama to rule, and remained in his hands until forcibly annexed by the Chinese under Chao-Erh-Feng in 1911.[33]

In the meantime, the sporadic fighting between the British and Tibetans on the borders resulted in a signing of an agreement between China and British on 17 March 1890 in

India. The important points of this agreement were firstly, that the British recognized Beijing's right to negotiate on Tibet's behalf. Secondly, the treaty allowed British control over the internal administration and foreign relations of Sikkim and stipulated that of the Teesta river should form the boundary between Sikkim and Tibet.[34] As Tibetans refused to recognize this boundary line, Lord Curzon formulated a new policy towards Tibet "...to cover not merely small questions of Sikkim frontier, but the entire question of our (British) future relations, commercial or otherwise with Tibet."[35] Unfortunately, no one from the Dalai Lama's side responded to this policy. When all attempts to communicate with the Dalai Lama and Tibet were exhausted on 8 January 1903, Lord Curzon wrote a letter to the Secretary of the State for India regarding the status of Tibet "Chinese suzerainty over Tibet is a constitutional fiction a political affectation which has only been maintained because of its conscience to both parties."[36]

Based on Charles Bell's note to the British Government regarding Russia's involvement in Tibet and so called secret deal between and China and Russia on Tibet, the British Government set Colonel Younghusband on a political mission to put relations with Tibet on a satisfactory footings. Later on, a political mission changed into military mission. Because of the military expedition of Younghusband, in Tibet, the Dalai Lama fled to Mongolia, leaving his seal to trusted priests. Nevertheless Younghusband managed to conquer Tibet, and made it sign the Anglo-Tibetan Treaty in September 1904. This treaty laid down the foundation of Britain's dealings with Tibet. The main terms of this treaty were, the Tibetan Government agreed to recognize the British protectorate over Sikkim, to promote trade between India, to set up three trade marts in Tibet and to prevent other foreigners exercising influence in Tibet.[37] The last term regarding foreigners influence could be related to Russia's interference in Tibet. However, at the closing ceremony of treaty signing, Colonel Younghusband, said that, "the British Government fully recognized the suzerainty of the Chinese Government and the British had not the least desire to supplant China in the suzerainty of Tibet."[38] However, to make a point were, the lack of a China's official's signature on the 1904 pact constituted a *de jure* change in Tibetan status.

Initially, the Chinese Government tried to revive its claim to be the sole medium of communication between the Government of India and Tibetans and to replace the Anglo-Tibetan Treaty by a new Agreement. But later on it was persuaded to accept the Lhasa convention which was signed at Peking in April, 1906. It secured the adhesion of China to the convention established with Tibet 1904. According to the convention (1906), a weakening China decided to insinuate itself once again into an influential position in Tibet.

In April 1905, once again Tibetans of the *Kham* province (*Khambas*), and the Lamas of great *Batang* monastery rose in open revolt and attacked the Chinese. In retaliation, the Chinese Government sent a general, Chao-Erh-Feng to suppress the rebellion using all types of merciless practices and harsh measures. After crushing the *Khambas* revolt, and conquering *Ba-Tang* monastery,

> *Chao* abolished the rank of native chiefs and appointed Chinese magistrates in their places, introduced new laws limiting the number of Lamas and depriving monasteries of their temporal power and inaugurated schemes for having the land cultivated by Chinese immigrants.[39]

As a reward for this, Chao was appointed as Imperial Commissioner for Tibet in March 1908. While doing so, the Chinese subjugated almost the whole of Tibet under its rule.

Towards, the end of 1909, Chao had several thousands of Chinese troops in Kham, preparing for march into Lhasa. When the Khambas complained to the Lhasa Government, the Dalai Lama told them that Chao didnot intend to do that and denied the request of Khambas to retaliate. On the contrary he told the Khambas not to take arms against its powerful neighbour and asked permission to seek negotiations with the Resident who was Chinese. The discouraged Tibetans made a telegraphic appeal through India to the foreign powers of Europe and the Chinese Government, but nobody responded. Finally, Chao marched into Tibet on 10 February 1910 and compelled the Dalai Lama to take asylum at the last minute. He reached India at Darjeiling on 21 February 1910 and was deposed on 25 February 1910 by an official device from Beijing Government observing that, "he has shown himself ....disobedient to the imperial commands and oppressive to the Tibetans. He is not fit to be a reincarnation of Buddha."[40]

The thirteenth Dalai Lama was in asylum in India for almost two years, and during his stay he petitioned India and Russia both for the aid and freedom from Chinese suzerainty over Tibet. With the outbreak of Chinese revolution in 1911, and the end of Manchurian Empire, the thirteenth Dalai Lama had realized that, Chinese suzerainty over Tibet was more fiction then fact. Hence, he and his followers began to think in terms of independent Tibet when China was at disadvantageous position. To do so, the Dalai Lama decided to return to his holy city of Lhasa in July 1912. Before his departure the British India Government once again reaffirmed that there could be no interference between Tibet and China on the part of HMG (His Majesty's Government) but advised the Dalai Lama before his departure:

> The Government of India wish [es] the Dalai Lama a safe and prosperous journey... The desire of the Government is to see the internal autonomy of Tibet under China's suzerainty, maintained without Chinese interference so long as treaty obligations are duly performed and cordial relations preserved between Tibet and India.[41]

However, after the revolution of 1911 at the domestic level in Tibet, there was chaos. According to an American missionary:

> There is no method of torture known and not practised on the Tibetans, slicing, skinning, boiling, tearing as under and all.... To sum up what China is doing here in eastern Tibet, the main

> things are collecting taxes, robbing, oppressing, confiscating and allowing her representatives to burn and loot and steal.[42]

So, after his arrival in Lhasa, the thirteenth Dalai Lama, declared "independence for Tibet" and then began a purge of his opponents. Pro-Han elements were sought out and punished, the expelled including thousands of monks. The pro-Chinese monasteries, estates and properties were confiscated and completely disbanded. On the other hand, he also tried to introduce some reforms, attacked opium use, smoking, and gambling. He created an 8,000 man standing army, tried to reform the penal and *ulag* systems, and began giving officials predetermined salaries and so on. Unfortunately, all these positive approaches and efforts of the Dalai Lama could not counteract the direct Chinese influence in Tibet and was far from obtaining the unanimous approval of the Tibetan population.[43]

Britain was not happy with Tibet's links with Russia and Japan. To reduce the Russia influence in Tibet, Britain determined to set the boundaries of Tibet and make Tibet a buffer state between China and India by placing a resident in Lhasa. To do so Britain threatened China saying it would not accept Chinese suzerainty over Tibet, and it would not recognize the new Chinese Republic.

Later on Britain insisted upon Sino-British negotiations in India, and the Dalai Lama also suggested conducting the proposed Sino-Tibet talks in India so that thereby a tripartite conference would be created. Initially China refused this idea but when Britain threatened that it would conduct the negotiation with Tibet without the Chinese representatives China agreed to the conference. The Conference began in October 1913, with Zhen Yutan representing China, Lonchan shatra from Tibet and the Indian Foreign Secretary, Sir Henry McMahon from Britain. The venue was Simla, strategically, it was changed from Darjeeling to Simla. The process of signing the pact began in April 1914, but it was finally signed on 3 July 1914 by McMahon. The pact was called the Simla Convention of July 1914, nullifying the earlier 1893, 1906 and

1908 pacts, while dividing Tibet into two parts : inner and outer.

The Chinese denounced the Simla convention as they did not gain anything by signing it except for a reaffirmation of their suzerainty. Moreover, the treaty offered no gains to Tibet whatsoever, except to escape the suzerainty of China. In other words Tibet gave up territory and switched suzerains from China to Britain.[44] It was done in the hope that British mission would fortify Tibet's case for independence but unfortunately this did not happen. Whereas British India achieved maximum benefits out of this convention.

> It set the India-Tibet frontier, east of Bhutan, along the crest of the Himalayas, in what came to be known as the McMahon Line, and resulted in the acquisition of 2,000 square miles of territory for the British empire.... In addition, Britain obtained exclusive trading rights, extra-territoriality and the right to station a resident in Lhasa.[45]

Practically, for many years, the Simla convention was not implemented due to unclear publications of maps and relevant documents and lack of activity to produce the original text and identical copies of the frontier border. However the convention did serve Britain's short-terms aims such as Tibet, for all intents and purposes, becoming a British protectorate; and China and Russia being effectively forced out of the area.[46]

Tibet as Buffer State (1914 -1949)

Although, the outbreak of World War I, (1914 – 1919) in Europe diverted Britain's attention from Tibet, it could not stop Charles Bell from achieving its objective: to bring Tibet within the British sphere of influence. After the war, Bell arrived at Lhasa in 1920 and suggested some socio-economic programmes for the development of Tibet. For instance, taking Bell's advice, the Dalai Lama increased the Tibetan army from 5,000 to 15,000; a telegraphic line was constructed from Gyantse to Lhasa; a small hydro-electric plant was built in the capital and a police force was established with the aid of Sikkimese Police officers. A British-style school was set up in

Gyantse in 1924.[47] In addition to this; the British offered the Tibetan nobility the privileges and pleasures of an advanced material technology.

Overwhelmed by these gestures by the British, the Dalai Lama told Bell, "all the people of Tibet and me have become of one mind and the British and Tibetan have become one family."[48] However certain sections of the Tibetan nobility were not happy with Britain's attitude towards Tibet as London officially stated to the Chinese that they saw Tibet as an autonomous state under the suzerainty of China."[49] This view was resented by many young Tibetans and monks. So they preferred to develop closer ties with China, the other reason could be the Tibetan nobility and monks had traditional ties and economic interests in China. Whereas in other parts of Tibet, especially in Kham and Amdo, the largely populated areas, fierce and independent nomads, could not be controlled by either Tibet (Lhasa) Government or the Chinese Government. Even Lhasa realized that and kept nominal control over their activities. No Tibetan official would go there to perform its function because of the war-like nature of the Kham people. "From 1911 to 1935 there were 400 to 500 major battles in the Sinkiang – Sichuan area (roughly Kham)... The local people fought equally against rule from Lhasa and rule from Beijing, they also often fought among themselves."[50] It is interesting to note after the death of the thirteenth Dalai Lama, in 1933 there was an uprising, an unsuccessful attempt to create a separate Kham state independent of Lhasa and Beijing. Khamas and Amdos achieved a short-lived victory but were quickly repelled by a combine Han and Tibetan force.[51]

As mentioned earlier, the Tibetan nobility and monks were interested in developing relations with China; the thirteenth Dalai Lama had regular correspondence with the new President of Republic of China, Yuan Shikai. During his life time, the Dalai Lama, continued to send learned Lamas to Buddhist temples in Beijing. These exchanges between the two states, paved the way for China to reconcile its relationship with Tibet. Moreover, the rift between the Dalai Lama and Panchen Lama, which led to the flight of the Panchen to China in 1924, gave an opportunity to the Chinese to interfere in Tibet's internal affairs.[52]

As a result of these developments, in 1930, the KMT Government for first time sent a mission to Lhasa headed by Ms. Liu, who was born to a Tibetan mother and a Chinese father, well-versed in both the languages, culture and traditions. This was the first delegation from the Chinese side, but it did not change the status of relationship but initiated a fruitful dialogue between the two. The second delegation of China could not reach Tibet because of the untimely death of the Chinese representative on his way. However, as a courtesy, the Dalai Lama personally took an interest in performing the last rituals at representative's funeral in Lhasa. This event was viewed by China as a positive response by Tibet to their efforts to establish an office in Lhasa.[53] The death of the thirteenth Dalai Lama in 1933, provided an opportunity to the Chinese Government, to send its delegation and pay its respects to the late Dalai Lama. However, the main purpose was to establish firm and cordial relations with Tibet, and to do so, the Chinese representative General Huang, began negotiations with the Tibetan officials over the border issue, trade and the status of the Panchen Lama.[54] As a result of these negotiations and exchanges by the end of April 1940, China established its "office of the commission of Mongolian and Tibetan affairs in Lassa"[55]

The Sino-Tibetan relations during the 1920 – 1940 periods (especially Tibet's tilting towards China) provoked the British into sending their political officer for Sikkim, Frederick Williamson to Lhasa to offer his good offices, indirectly to reassert its control in Tibet. Successor of F. Williamson, Basil J. Gould came to Lhasa with a new British Trade Agent and military advisor, Hugh Richardson in 1936.[56] The main purpose was to offer military training to the Tibetans and at the same time, establish a permanent office like China, had done, in Lhasa.[57] But the Tibetan Government denied this status to the British Government as it would be unwarranted interference in its foreign affairs, and decided to follow its traditional policy of isolation.

After the death of the thirteenth Dalai Lama in 1933, when the fourteenth Dalai Lama was established on 21 February 1940 no confirmation of the appointment was sought from China[57] under the pretext that Tibet was independent since 1911. At this time, the Chinese mission attended the inauguration ceremony and treated on equal footing with the British envoy. It described this a, "a deliberate action designed to convey the impression that both were representatives of foreign countries."[58] The fourteenth Dalai Lama during his inauguration received his official name as *The Holy One, The Gentle Glory, Powerful in Speech, Pure in Mind, of Divine, Wisdom, Holding the Faith wide as a Ocean*

In addition to this, the Tibetan looked at World War II (1939 – 43) as an opportunity to exert its independent status. To demonstrate this, the Tibetan Government in the summer of 1943, set up the Bureau of Foreign Affairs under the *Ko-nsia (Kashag)* and informed the office of the Mongolian and Tibetan Affairs Commission in Tibet that its business should henceforth be conducted with the Bureau and no longer with the *Ko- nsia* directly.[59] The other motive behind this Bureau was, if relations with foreign countries could be formalized, these nations would in turn recognize and support the Tibetan claim to sovereignty.[60] In the meantime, in September 1942, an American Military Mission paid a visit to Lhasa from India and from there to China. It had two objectives. First, to explore the new route through which supplies could be dispatched to China from India during the war and secondly to establish the first official contacts between Tibet and U.S.A.[61]

Sino-Tibetan relations were strained during the war, as the Pro-British youth group came into power who refused to recognize Chinese superiority [control] over Tibet. Hence, China decided to follow a policy of low profile and appointed its representative Shen-Tsung-Lien in August 1944. He hold a series of talks with the Tibetan Government but this whole exercise was futile as the Tibetans did not find any common ground with the Chinese. So, to further its efforts to win over Tibet, China made it clear to the Tibetans that they would receive without any restriction, a high degree of autonomy. Moreover, the Chinese Government decided to assist Tibet in political and economic development. To quote *Chiang-Kai-Shek* 's statement of August 25, 1945:

> If and when the Tibetans attain the stage of complete self-reliance in political and economic conditions, the Chinese Government would like to take the same attitude as it did toward outer Mongolia, by supporting their independence. However, Tibet should be able to maintain and promote its own independent position in order that the historical tragedy of Korea might not be repeated.[62]

But the relationship between Tibet and China did remain unchanged. Nevertheless by the end of 1945 – 46, when China emerged as a member of the Big Five Powers. Tibet's attitude to China changed a little bit, not friendly but less hostile. Later on, in the year 1947, a Tibetan delegation attended the proceedings of China's National Assembly and took active part in drafting the constitution, which determines the legal status of Tibet. When the assembly came to discuss the proposal, "Tibet's local autonomy shall be decided by law," they demanded this article be deleted. Finally a compromise solution was reached whereby the wording was changed to "Tibet's autonomy shall be duly guaranteed.[63]

In addition to this, the invitation to the *Asian Relation Conference at New Delhi* in April 1947 provided an opportunity for Tibet to assert its independent status. During this conference its flag was flown along with those of other nations and the maps used indicated that Tibet was a separate state from China. At this Conference India respected Tibet as a separate state and its status as a buffer state between India and China.

On 15 August 1947, India's independence was viewed by Tibetans as an incentive to a greater degree of independence and self-government in a real manner. Tibet had hopes that independent India would not follow its predecessor's policy towards it, and would co-operate with courteous gestures. Very soon, Tibet realized this was an illusion, when independent India decided to follow the policies set by the previous Government (British). The policy, which was best summed up in 1943 in a War Cabinet Memo:

> We have promised the Tibetan government to support them in maintaining the practical autonomy of Tibet, which is of importance to the security of India... On the other hand over alliance with China makes it difficult to give effective material support to Tibet... at some stage discussion...Is probably inevitable... [Since] our recognition of China's suzerainty over Tibet is a handicap, in that the Chinese Government can argue that suzerainty involves some degree of control.[64]

Independent India reiterated the same policy towards Tibet which has its significance even today. Thus, in 1947 India took over the British mission in Lhasa and the trade agencies in the other population centers. The only change was, Hugh Richardson who on 14 August was a British Civil Servant representing Britain in Lassa, became on 15 August, an Indian Civil Servant representing New Delhi in Lhasa.

Two years later, a great upheaval shook China when the Kuomingtang regime collapsed in the war against the communists. The emergence of the People's Republic of China on 1 October 1949 led by the communists, left no doubt that they were not prepared to concede Tibet anything comparable to an independent status. To prove this policy of China one can quote Mao's statement during his proclamation on the same day he said, "The Chinese People's Republic would wage a war of liberation to the very end' and 'liberate all the territory of China."[65]

During the same period, in 1949, the Tibetan Government made a last desperate attempt to declare independence. The Kuomingtang mission in Lhasa was pushed out and the Tibetan Government declared that Tibet was an independent and neutral country anxious to live in friendship and amity with China and India.

Red China's Aggression of Tibet (1949-1959)

Due to the fear of Chinese communists to establish a foothold in Lhasa the *Kashag*, the Tibetan cabinet, expelled the Chinese mission and all Han residents from Tibet. Most of them were connected with the Chinese National Government, including those working in the radio station and hospital and the teachers of Chinese primary schools, in Lhasa and Gyantse. This decision of *Kashag* communicated to Chen Xizhang the acting director of the Mongolian and Tibetan affairs officer in Lhasa on 8 July 1949. Moreover, fearing that the Chinese might organize a protest in the streets of Lhasa, the *Kashag* imposed a curfew until all the Chinese had left.[66] When, the same decision was communicated to the General Chiang-Kai-Shek, both, the Nationalist and Communist strongly resented this decision and asked the Tibetan Government to rectify its decisions.

Especially the communists came up with the accusation that, 'imperialist' means British and their 'running dogs' means India of manufacturing so-called anti-communist incidents in Tibet and of trying to turn the 1.2 million sq. mn into a colony.[67] In an editorial, on 2 September 1949, the *Hsin Hwa Pao* remarked:

> The affair of expelling the Han Chinese and Kuoming tang [Guomingdoang] officials at Lhasa was a plot undertaken by the local Tibetan authorities through the instigation of the British imperialists and their lackey the Nehru administration of India. The purpose of this anti-Chinese affair is to prevent the people in Tibet from being liberated by the Chinese people, Liberation Army.[68]

The act of expulsion of the Chinese mission implied that the Chinese communists became convinced that foreign powers had penetrated Tibet and had stored up hostility towards them. Hence the Chinese were thinking how to control Tibet and bring it under its communist regime. In the meanwhile, a month after the communists came to power in China, the Tibetan Foreign Bureau wrote to the British Foreign Secretary, Ernest Bevin seeking support. The Foreign Bureau enclosed the copy of a letter that had been sent to Chairman Mao, which declared that Tibet was an independent country and that the new government should observe the established boundary. Whereas the letter to Bevin pointed out the growing threat of communism and stated : "we would be most grateful if you would please consider extensive aid in respect of requirements for civil and military purposes and kindly let us have a favourable reply at your earliest possible opportunity."[69]

This decision was taken by the Tibet Government according to the far-sighted approach adopted by its National Assembly. Firstly, the *Kashag* sought admission to the United Nations and second, missions were dispatched to Nepal, India, U.S.A. and UK to seek support for Tibetan independence.

So on 3 December 1949, the *Kashag* sent a telegram to the British Government requesting support for the admission of Tibet into the United Nations. In response the British Government stated that the admission of Tibet if the UNO was subject to the approval, not mercy of the UNO Assembly but also of the Security Council where the veto could be used by the other two members, China and Russia.[70] It was a clear hint from Britain that it was not going to help in this regard. Whereas the GOI replied, 'that the GOI had not received a request from the Tibetan Government and therefore it saw no reason to act.'[71] Moreover, India did not want to get involved in this matter because, interference in Tibetan affairs means 'lending colour to Peking radio allegation of Anglo-Indian ganging up over Tibet by our acting together in this way.'[72] The Indian Ambassador to China, Sardar K.M. Pannikar, had advised that India should 'wash her hands completely of Tibet.'[73]

All these developments on the issue of independent status of Tibet and its admission in UNO, gave an impression to the Tibetan Government that there was no one who could support its cause, especially, Britain and India, who had lost their strategy as well as economic interests in Tibet. So, they had to fight on their own.

In view of this deterioration in relationship between the United States and Communist China, the Tibetan government decided to approach the United States for assistance and aid. Moreover Tibet was aware of America's concerns of expansion by the USSR and Communism in Asia, so it felt, USA might help her to seek and protect its independence. Washington gave a positive reply saying: "if Tibet intended to resist Communist aggression and needed help the US government was prepared to assist in procuring material and would finance each aid."[74] However, America was categorical, that they were willing to provide this aid in the event of Communist attack. This stand by the Americans led to confusion in the minds of Tibetans about its policy towards Tibet. Probably, America's great involvement in the Korean crisis compelled it to take this stand. Finally, the Tibetans had no help from anyone.

As mentioned earlier, when the Chinese communists came to power in 1949, Radio Peking announced that the task of the People's Liberation Army (PLA) for 1950 was to liberate Taiwan, Hainan and Tibet. Mao served notice on the world that he also intended to bring Tibet under his power. To do that, on 7 October 1950, 40,000 Chinese troops attacked Eastern Tibet's provincial capital Chamdo, (a strategically important gate to enter into Tibet from the Chinese side) from eight directions and defeated the small Tibetan army.[75] More than 4000 Tibetan soldiers were killed in this attack. Later on, Tibet's request for assistance and aid from the foreign powers such as India, Britain, France and America, annoyed the Chinese, as did the American positive reply to Tibetan request, viewed by China as a threat to their existence. Hence on 8 November 1950 the Chinese South-West Military Administrative Committee and Military proceeded to order the PLA to enter Tibet for the purpose of assisting the Tibetan people to free themselves from aggression forever.[76]

As Tibetans were aware of their limitations to fight against China, the Dalai Lama sent a message to the PLA in Chamdo indicating that "he sincerely wanted to restore the friendship between the Tibetan and the Han."[77] So, he authorized the delegates in Beijing to begin negotiations.

In India the overall reaction was surprise and shock for the Indian leaders. Especially Sardar Vallabhbhai Patel the then Deputy Prime Minister and Home Minister on 9 November 1950, who said :

> To use the sword against the traditionally peace-loving Tibetan people was unjustified. No other country in the world is as peace-loving as Tibet. The Chinese government did not follow India's advice to settle the Tibetan issue peacefully. They marched their armies into Tibet and explained this action by talking foreign interest intriguing in Tibet against China. But this fear is unfounded.[78]

On 23 May 1951, these two representatives finally signed the Agreement of the Central People's Government and the Local Government of Tibet, or as it is commonly known, the Seventeen-Point Agreement. The Agreement declared that "the Tibetan people shall unite and drive out imperialist aggressive forces from Tibet and shall return to the big family or the Motherland – The People's Republic of China."[79]

In addition to this, the Agreement went on to promise:

> the maintenance or the status quo in the Tibetan regional government structure as well as in the internal position and authority of the Dalai Lama but called on the Lhasa Government actively to assist the People's Liberation Army to enter, and consolidate the national defense, while permitting 'autonomy under the unified leadership of the Central People's Government'. Tibetan troops were to be reorganised into the People's Liberation Army, and all foreign affairs to be handled by Peking.[80]

During the invasion, the Dalai Lama who had fled to Yatung, after a long discussions and negotiation, returned to Lhasa. After his return, the bulk of aristocracy returned as well. The return of the Dalai Lama remains a puzzle, as he had on opportunity to come out of Tibet safely and fight back with the support from other foreign powers and struggle for independence. According to George Patterson, an American, who claims to have been a participant in these events, "the Dalai Lama was 'desparate' to leave Tibet for India to exile.

His belongings had already been sent ahead; his family was anxiously awaiting from in Kalimpong, India; and Heinrich Harrer had even drawn up a map of the route to be travelled south."[81]

It is interesting to note, T. Norbu, the elder brother the Dalai Lama, who had escaped to Kalimpong quietly during the invasion, negotiated on behalf of the Dalai Lama with Americans and reached a four-point agreement. George Patterson, who was instrumental behind this, communicated with the Dalai Lama. Briefly the terms were:

1. On his escaping from Tibet, the U.S. would agree to support the Dalai Lama and one hundred and twenty members of his government for an indefinite period of any country of the Dalai Lama's choosing, but it was thought advisable that the country should be in the east.
2. The U.S. would take up the matter of China's aggression against Tibet, and Tibet's plea for help, in the U.N.
3. The U.S. provide finance for whatever was required in Tibet's fight for freedom from the Chinese.
4. Any question of military assistance would have to be left for future discussion, but on his arrival in India the Dalai Lama should approach the Indian Government for help, and when this was refused, as it would be, he was to request the Indian Government for permission to approach any other country willing to help."[82]

But all of these commitments were predicated on the condition that the Dalai Lama leave Tibet and publicly repudiate the Seventeen-Point Agreement. It shows that America had also indirectly, recognized the agreement as a valid legal document between Tibet and China.

By September 1951, the PLA reached Lhasa and other major Tibetan population centres and repeatedly violated the terms of the agreement, unleashing increasing repression in Tibet. Gradually, the Chinese army marched into other parts of Tibet; particularly it established military camps in the provinces of Amdo and Kham and so brought almost all of

Tibet under its control. This led to acute problems of food supply; moreover, the Chinese army demanded a lion's share of the available grain to feed its men. The Tibetan people protested about the forcible requisitions that quickly drove prices sky-high and anti-Chinese posters sprang up around the city.[83]

In addition to this, Tibet was divided into three administrative zones, each under separate authority of the Dalai Lama, the Panchen Lama, third being a Chinese general.[84] These division of Tibet curtailed the administrative authority of the Dalai Lama and brought almost all Tibet under Chinese control. In this way, the Chinese declared a peacefully liberated Tibet, by 28 April 1952.

As a result of this Agreement of 1951, Tibet witnessed many unfortunate developments (social-economic-political) during the 1951-1954 period. Once the Panchen Lama arrived in Lhasa, the authorities consistently pursued the policy of building up his official stature so as to present him to the Tibetan masses of least as the Dalai Lama's equal.[85]

To do that, the Chinese government stature officially treated them as on par in all matters affecting Tibet giving them similar honors, and position at various function and public bodies. Moreover,, China followed various policies, ways and means to of weakening the Dalai Lama's position temporal as well as religious, and discredited the important aspects Tibet's socio-economic and political system.

According to some reports China also made an attempt to fly the Chinese flag over the Potala Palace, the official residential place of the Dalai Lama, but this request was refused by the latter. The Military Mission in Lhasa opened a "cultural department" to indoctrinate Tibetans in Marxist Philosophy and launched a comprehensive information programme to familiarize the local people with the Communist manifesto and the 1951 treaty.[86] China consolidated all economic activities and put them under its control by opening a People's Bank of China in Lhasa. Thus local financial institutions of Tibet were almost captured by the Chinese. Tibetans protested against this encroachment on its traditions and institutions by the Central Government of China. This culminated in growing hostility between the Tibetans and the Chinese, and finally erupted in the emergence of an anti-communist secret 'People's Committee' (1953), the first Tibetan national political party. It has organized widespread demonstrations by its adherents and armed uprisings in provinces of Kham and Amdo.

The Tibetan resistance apparently forced China to withdraw some of its troops and relinquish some of its controls as well as to reconsider its policy towards Tibetan people. On the other hand, although only initially so, GOI was reluctant to recognize Chinese control and invasion of Tibet in 1950. But according to the Seventeen-Point Agreement of 1951, on 15 September 1952, it had officially announced that henceforth any relations with Lhasa would be conducted through Beijing. Furthermore, the Indian diplomatic mission in Lhasa became a Consulate General, while the Trade Agencies (in Gartok, Gyantse and Yatung) were to come under the jurisdiction of the Consulate, thereby recognizing that Tibet was a part of the PRC.[87] Thus, India agreed to the changed status of Tibet from an independent to an autonomous state of China, but did not accept the Chinese sovereignty over Tibet till it had signed the Panchsheel Agreement with China on 27 April 1954.

According to this Agreement, the GOI formally recognized Tibet as a region of China. In other words, India accepted the Chinese Claim on Tibet. Pandit Nehru might have agreed for this agreement due to many compulsions which are discussed in the later part of this paper. But one cannot deny that one of the reasons could be too much faith and trust in Mao-Tse-Tung, who had promised that Tibet would enjoy autonomy, which no other province of China had. But it was mere propaganda which India realized much later in 1955-58, when it eyewitnessed the Chinese atrocities on the Tibetan population.

In reference to the 1954 Agreement, it is very important to note where H.E. Richardson mentioned in his speech at ICWA, New Delhi on 2 December 1960, he said:

> I,should draw attention to one consequence of it. There is tendency among some Indian writers to treat as marking a break away from the proceeding regime in its voluntary surrender of certain territorial rights in Tibet. That may look very fine in political speeches and so on, but as a matter of historical accuracy I suggest that it needs to be tested by the scrutiny with the facts. There had been an excellent opportunity to surrender those rights, if they were so distasteful, in 1947 or anytime before the Chinese invasion of Tibet... when the rights were eventually surrendered in 1954 they were handed over, not to the Tibetans who had willingly granted them in 1914 but to the Chinese who had seized Tibet and had made the rights no longer tenable.[88]

Once GOI had surrendered its special relationship and rights with Tibet, the Chinese started showing their true colours. For instance, just before that winter out break of 1955, Chinese introduced the land reforms in Tibet, which meant the collectivization of Tibetan land, the farms, cattle and sheep owned by the lamaseries and the monasteries were converted into farm — co-operatives. These reforms confirmed the belief that the Chinese were out to destroy the Tibetan way of life, which was intolerable for any Tibetan. "Matters were aggravated by the introduction of Chinese paper money and by Chinese borrowings from Tibetan resources of gold and silver".[89] Attacks on the position of the Dalai Lama, on the religious doctrine and religious establishments such as monasteries led feelings of resentment, the atmosphere being made even worse by economic difficulties like, when the Chinese sent troops to Lhasa, within a short time smuggling of food was started, prices went up and hard feelings went up with them.[90]

As a result, the revolt broke out in Tibet in the winter of 1955-56. The guerrilla units organised by the Khampas attacked the Chinese positions with extreme savagery. So the Chinese government decided to stamp out the rebellions by any means whatsoever, and crushed the revolt in blood by January 1956. The next step towards integrating Tibet was taken on 22 April 1956, with the creation of the preparatory committee for the Autonomous Region of Tibet, a body whose avowed purpose was to assimilate Tibet and cast it in the Chinese administrative mould.[91] To do so, Chinese declared Tibet as a thinly populated area and encouraged thousands of Chinese people of Han origin to settle down in Tibet; these later occupied all the important posts in Tibetan administration and thus sidelined the nationals of Tibet.

In November 1956, when the Dalai Lama along with his officials, visited Delhi during this time, a group of self-exiled Tibetans prevented the Dalai Lama's return to Tibet. Moreover he, himself foresaw what would happen in Tibet within a few years, so he informed Nehru that, he had no desire to return to his homeland. He asked for either political asylum in India or assistance in acquiring a similar status in any Buddhist nation. Nehru, pleased with the slogan of *Hindi-Chini- Bhai-Bhai*, displeased by this turn of events, tried to convince the Tibetan that he would be more useful in Lhasa, working closely with Beijing and sustaining the morale of his people. Thus, he was pursuaded to return to Tibet after Nehru had obtained what seemed reasonable assurances from Chou-en-Lai that the Chinese would observe their treaty obligations towards the Tibetans.[92] To do so, the Chinese officially announced the postponement of the reforms which they had been preparing and they actually did recall some of their officials and troops from Lhasa. But at the same time they committed barbarous deeds between 1956 to 1958. The Chinese tortured and suppressed the Tibetan clergy and destroyed hundreds of temples and monasteries. The Chinese army emptied entire arsenals of weapons to intimidate the local populations; Tibetans were crucified, burned alive, decapitated and dismembered. Entire villages were razed and wiped off the map. Despite this, the guerillas did not lay down their arms. On the contrary, the atrocities on Tibetans compelled them to raid the PLA positicns in Tibet. Particularly, the Khampa warriors, who left their homes just to revolt against the Chinese rule in central Tibet, destroyed Chinese supply of convoys to annihilate a garrison of 3,000 men and arrived within 60 miles of the capital Lhasa. They were just beyond the control of the Chinese. The Chinese then requested the Dalai Lama to allow his Tibetan troops to suppress the guerillas, which was refused by the latter. He made the excuse that no Tibetan would fight against his fellow countrymen. According to Richardson, the Chinese seem to have decided to remove the Dalai Lama from Tibet. Hence on 1 March 1959, he was invited by the Chinese when he was at his Summer Palace at Norbulingka to attend a theatrical performance of a PLA camp near Lhasa. In response, the Dalai made some excuse and due to his pre-engaged religious activities, refused to visit PLA camps. On March 7, 1959, once again he was approached by the Chinese who requested him to select a day on which he could attend the performance, 10 March being selected. The Dalai Lama felt suspicious about the invitation as it had not came through the proper channel. Moreover he was asked to come with a handful of unarmed bodyguards. The visit was kept secret. He wrote in 1959:

> A rumour spread at once throughout the city that the Chinese had made a plan to kidnap me. During the evening and night of the 9th of the March, excitement grew, and by the morning most of the people to Lhasa and decided spontaneously to prevent my visit to the Chinese camp at any cost.[93]

On 10 March, the crowd gathered around the Norbulingka and did not allow him to come out, instead three ministers were sent on his behalf to the PLA camps. On the same day, the important decisions were taken by the Tibetans at the Norbulingka institute. It was resolved to renounce the Seventeen-Point Agreement and call for the expulsion of all the Han from Tibet and declare an independent Tibet. From 10 March 1959, within a week's time, by 17 March 1959, evening at 4 p.m. the Dalai claims to have heard the two mortar shells, fired from the direction of the Chinese PLA military camp, which led him to take a hasty decision, and flee from Tibet. By 10 p.m. that evening he left his palace, dressed as a simple monk and crossed the Indian frontiers, along with his 13,000 followers on 31 March 1959.

References

1. In the Tawang region of Arunachal Pradesh many Tibetans were settled almost a century ago and hold Indian citizenship
2. Chanakya Sen, *Tibet Disappears*, (Bombay: Asia Publishing House, 1960), p.2.
3. Quoted in Chanakya Sen, n.2. pp.14 – 15
4. Bon-Po, a folk religion of Tibet, after fighting a desperate battle with Buddhism for many years, began to decline in the 12th and 13th centuries.
5. Chanakya Sen, n.2. p.2.A. Tom Grunfeld, *The Making of Modern Tibet*, (Bombay : Oxford University Press, 1987), p.24.
6. Ibid.
7. However in modern times, many Tibetans find that their scriptures are based on the Sanskrit language and are similar to Oriya Script.
8. *Tibet: The Facts, A Report prepared by the Scientific Buddhist Association (London) for the UNCHR*, (Dharamsala; TYBA, 1990) p.2.
9. Ibid.
10. A. Tom Grunfeld, n.6. p.9.
11. Ibid.
12. Ibid.
13. George N. Patterson, *Tibet in Revolt* (London: Faber and Faber, 1960), p. 41.
14. Ibid, p.42.
15. Quoted in Ibid.
16. George N. Patterson, n.13, p.18.
17. Ibid, Alto, See *Tibet : The Facts* n.9. P.3.
18. Ibid, pp. 18 – 19.
19. From that time Tibet was ruled by the Sakya Lamas as a theocracy. See, George N. Patterson, n.14, P.19. For details, also see, Chapter II, "Tibet As A Vassal State" in Tieh-Tseng Li, *The Historical Status of Tibet* (New York: King's Crown Press, 1956), pp. 18 – 32.

20. Since then the Yellow Hats are *Ge-luk-pas* have been the most powerful sect in Tibet and the present Dalai Lama is its head. For details see, Grunfeld, n.5, pp. 37 – 42.
21. George N. Patterson, n.14, P.21.
22. Quoted in Tieh-Tseng Li, *The Historical Status of Tibet*, (New York : Kings Crown Press, 1956), P. 34.
23. Ibid; p.35
24. Ibid; p.36
25. Ibid, p.37
26. George N. Patterson, n. 14, p.22
27. Ibid.
28. Quoted in Ibid, p.25
29. Ibid.
30. Ibid, p.26
31. Ibid, pp. 26 – 27
32. Ibid, p.27
33. Ibid, p.28
34. Ibid.
35. Ibid.
36. Ibid.
37. Ibid, p.29
38. Tieh n.23 p.66
39. A.T. Grunfeld, n.6 p.60
40. Tieh, n.23, p.127.
41. A.T. Grunfeld, n.6. p.63
42. Ibid.
43. Ibid, p.65
44. Ibid.
45. Ibid, p.66
46. Ibid, p.68,
47. Ibid.
48. Ibid.
49. Ibid.
50. Ibid.
51. Since 1924 the Pachem Lama has been traditional rival of the Dalai Lama and an ally of China and an instrumental of China's Tibet policy. For details see, Chanakya Sen, n.2. p.11

52. Tieh – Li,
53. Ibid.
54. A.T. Grunfeld, n.6. P.72.
55. The British Government was interested in providing British military aid and training for the Tibetans. This policy was strongly propounded since the F. Williamson period and continued by H.E. Richardson who served as Political officer in Tibet (1947 – 1950).
56. Tieh – Li, n.23, p.72.
57. George N. Patterson, n. 14 , p.55
58. In 1926, The Tibetan Government already setup the Foreign Office, mainly to regulate and conduct the increasing official business with foreign countries. Particularly the Mongols and the Nepalese. See, Ram Rahul, *The Government of Tibet (1912 – 1933), International Studies*, (New Delhi), Vol. IV, No.2, October 1962, pp.172 – 173.
59. Tieh–Li, n.23, p.186.
60. A.T. Grunfeld. n.6. p.74
61. Chanakya Sen, n.2 p.12
62. Tieh–Li, n.23, p.190
63. Ibid, p.191
64. A.T. Grunfeld, n.6, p.82.
65. Selected Speeches and Writings of Mao-Tse-Tung on October 1, 1949.
66. Tsering Shakya, *The Dragon in the Land of Snows: A History of Modern Tibet Since 1947*, (London : Pimlico, 1999) P.9.
67. Ibid.
68. It was H.E. Richardson suggestion to expel the Chinese mission. Even he was preparing some of the Tibetans to fight the battle militarily and accordingly he had given fire arms to them. For details see, Tsering Shakya, n.67 and Tieh–Li, no 23.
69. Tsering Shakya, n.67 p.17
70. Ibid
71. Ibid
72. A.T. Grunfeld n.6 p.105
73. Ibid

74. George N. Patterson n.14, p.78.
75. Ibid
76. A.T. Grunfeld, n.6, p.106.
77. George N. Patterson, n. 14, p.82.
78. George Ginsburgs and Michael Mathos, *Tibet's Admistrations in the Transition Period, 1951 – 54, Pacific Affairs* (Canada) Vol. XXXII No .II, June 1959, pp.171-172
79. Ibid.
80. Ibid.
81. Ibid, p.172
82. A.T. Grunfeld, n.5. p.113
83. H.E. Richardson, *Tibet Since 1950, India Quarterly*, (New Delhi), Vol. XVII No.2, April – June 1961, p.131
84. Ibid, p.133
85. George Ginsburg and Michael Mathos, *Tibet Administration during Interrgnum 1954 – 1959 Pacific Affairs*, Vol.XXXII No.III September 1959, pp.249 – 267.
86. P.A. Donnet, *Tibet : Survival in Question* (Delhi : Oxford University Press, 1992) p.25.
87. Dalai Lama in his speech on April, 1, 1959.
88. H.E. Richardson, n.84, p.134.
89. A.T. Grunfeld, n.6, p.116.
90. H.E. Richardson, n.84, p.134.
91. Ibid.
92. Quoted, A.T. Grunfeld, n.6, p.130.

3

SURVIVAL IN EXILE

As mentioned earlier, in 1949, as soon as Communist China came into existence, it declared its policy to liberate Tibet and to do so the Chinese army marched into Tibet and defeated the small and ill-equipped Tibetan army in the year 1950. As a result, the nation-wide resistance by Tibetans culminated in the Tibetan National Uprising in Lhasa on 10 March 1959, demanding total withdrawal of China from Tibet. The Tibetan National Uprising of 1959 made Chinese furious and it sent its army once again into Tibet. This time, the Chinese army ruthlessly crushed the uprising. About 87,000 Tibetans were killed in the Lhasa region alone, monks and nuns being a prime target. As a result, on 17 March 1959, His Holiness Dalai Lama along with his 13,000 followers escaped from Lhasa and sought political asylum in India. On 31 March 1959, he arrived at Chuthangmo, an Indian check-post, in the border and from there he has reached Tezpur (Assam).

Asylum in India

After the Dalai Lama's flight on 17 March 1959, the first report of an uprising broadcast by the *Voice of America* was on 22 March 1959.[1] The reason was, Americans were very much involved in the rebellion led by *Khampas* and they were supporting them with aid and weapons, particularly through the Gumingtong Government. However, they were neither associated in any way with the flight of the Dalai Lama, nor aware of it.[2] The Indian press, *The Times of India* dated 22 March 1959, reported the news of "the fighting in Lhasa, has been received with great concern in New Delhi and further information is likely to be sought from the Government by the Members of Parliament."[3] Prime Minister Nehru was extremely cautious while replying in the Indian Parliament on this issue. He described the clash in Tibet as "A clash of wills". To quote his speech in the Lok Sabha on 23 March 1959, first time after the flight of the Dalai Lama, "This is a difficult and delicate situation and we should avoid doing anything which will worsen it. We have no intention of interfering in the internal affairs of China with whom we have friendly relations."[4] This view was expressed by Nehru mainly on the basis of the Five Principles (*Panchsheel*) Agreement, signed in 29 April 1954, which also promises *non-interference* as one of the core its principles and India abided by it. However, at the same time Nehru had different considerations for the Tibetans. He was positive on granting political asylúm to the Dalai Lama. To support his decision in Parliament he said:

> ...there is a long tradition of cultural and religious ties between India and Tibet region of China. In this region lie many places of pilgrimage which are considered holy by both Hindus and Buddhists and large numbers of our people visit them every year. The Dalai Lama who we had the honour and pleasure of receiving in our country in 1956 – 57, is held in high veneration by our people and we hope he is safe. We earnestly trust that the present troubles will be resolved peacefully.[5]

On 31 March 1959, the Dalai Lama arrived at Chuthangmo, an Indian check-post, on the border, and from there he reached Tezpur (Assam). After his safe arrival in India at the beginning of April 1959, few Tibetans who had settled in India at Kalimpong for last few decades, approached Nehru and submitted a four point memorandum requesting that,

> (1) GOI should seek some form of guarantee from China for the personal safety of the Dalai Lama; (2) refugees should

> be allowed to enter India freely; (3) India should send a mercy mission with medical supplies and (4) India should sponsor the Tibetan case at the United Nations.[6]

In response, Nehru made it clear, that India was not in a position to intervene and in fact would not like to take any steps which might aggravate the situation there [in Tibet]'[7] Moreover, it seems that Nehru was pre-occupied on the issue of Tibet. To mention here prior to the Tibetan delegation's request for help, at one occasion, on 30 March 1959, he said, "...it was patent from the strictly practical point of view, even apart from sentiment, that we could not do anything in Tibet either in law, constitutionally or practically."[8] This opinion of Nehru came as a response to the Indian public's reaction to the Tibetan issue. Many opposition parties such as the Jan Sangh, and the Hindu Mahasabha organized demonstrations in major cities in India and the Praja Socialist Party declared 29 March as "Tibet Day". Even some of the members from his own party, the Congress Party criticized Nehru's policy on Tibet. But Nehru was firm, one can make out from his answer to Shri Naushir Bharucha and Shri Mohammed Imman in the Indian Parliament on 30 March 1959.

> One has to see the difficult situation as it is and not merely create conditions which make it more difficult to deal with the situation or deal with the persons seeking political asylum. There it is whatever I say in regard to that will make it more difficult for these people, I say. So that, on the one side there is this feeling of a certain kinship, if I may use that word, cultural kinship between the people of India and the people of Tibet. That of course, does not mean that we interfere in Tibet, in any way.[9]

In view of the nature of world politics, one can argue that, India's policy of non-interference in the Tibetan affairs was a well-calculated diplomacy and influenced by the implications of the Cold War in Asia. Along with China, the two superpowers America and Soviet Russia were both curious on the developments in Tibet. As Soviet Russia had a direct adjacent border with China, her intentions were either to help the Chinese to grab Tibet and stop American influence in the region, or extend communism further in Asia, as they had succeeded in doing in the Far-East and Eastern Europe, Hungary and Rumania. On the other hand, America was already stepped into the Gumingtong region of China and the Khampa region of Tibet since 1945 – 46 for trade reasons. The Khampa rebels who were fierce nomads revolted against the Chinese rule in 1949, 1951 and 1955 were supported by America with arms and assistance.

Chiang-Kai Shek, facilitated American to serve its interest of containing communism further in Asia, especially in Tibet. The other factors which might have influenced Nehru's two-fold policy on Tibet as mentioned earlier, were granting political asylum to the Dalai Lama but not to interfere into Tibetan region of China. Firstly, being a non-aligned country, India decided to remain out of the power conflict and follow its own policy. Whereas Pakistan, with whom India had hostile relations had joined hands with America and signed a military pact with it in 1952. This US- Pak military alliance and hostility between India and Pakistan intensified India's fear of dragging herself into dawn of the Cold War, which would have been irrational decision. As a result, India did not acknowledge the American role in Tibet, and was reluctant to provide any opportunity to use its territory to enter Tibet. Secondly, Nehru must have foreseen, once the Americans established their base, economic or military, this will have direct effect on India as Americans sitting in Tibet would monitor, possibly would control the activities on Indian territory, Pakistan and China. In other words it would be like welcoming America to expand its imperialist policy in the subcontinent. Thirdly, it is a well known fact that Nehru was a staunch anti-imperialist and had a softcorner towards the communists. Therefore one can see Nehru's policy towards Tibet was not to antagonize either China or Russian. This was reflected in the debate in Parliamentary sessions. That is why, Nehru's Tibet policy was under severe criticism by opposition political parties including his own but except for the communists who criticized Tibetan rebellions as reactionary. The Communist Party of India issued a statement on the Tibetan situation on 31 March 1959. "It expressed the satisfaction that China had successfully scotched the imperialist plot in Tibet. It repeated the Peking declaration that the Tibetan rebellion was reactionary."[10]

Although the Dalai Lama along with his followers crossed the Indian border on 31 March 1959, Nehru made it an official announcement only on 3 April 1959 in the Lok Sabha. In the meantime, he had personally met the Dalai Lama on 1 April 1959 at Tezpur and confirmed his safe asylum in India. It shows that Nehru had taken care and precaution on the issue, as he was aware of the sensitivity of the event. In Parliament he said;

> The facts are that on April 1, day before yesterday morning, we received a message from Shillong dated March 31 evening, that an emissary with a message from the Dalai Lama had arrived on our border check post; *Chutamgtu* in NEFA (North East Frontier Agency). The emissary had arrived there on March 29 stating the Dalai Lama had requested political asylum and that he (Dalai Lama) was expected to reach the border on March 30. We received the message on April 1, the same evening a message was received by us again from Shillong, dated April 1, that the Dalai Lama with a small party of eight had crossed into our territory on the evening of March 31.[11]

It is interesting to note that excluding western scholars and a few Tibetan scholars, like *Tsering Shakya*, leading Tibetan origin author maintains that, the role of CIA or connection between America and his elder brother *Gyalo Thondup* became useful to seek political asylum in India.[12] Using a hand-cracked Morse radio, Athar and Lhotse, members of CIA trained Tibetan resistance, sent a message to Washington asking for political asylum in India for the Dalai Lama. A senior CIA officer, John Greaney a Tibet specialist, put through an emergency call to Washington and within four hours, the CIA's man in New Delhi sent a wire back to Washington, saying that the Indian Prime Minister, Jawaharlal Nehru had kindly granted asylum to the Dalai Lama and his followers.[13]

Due to the political asylum given to the Dalai Lama, the Chinese Government accused India of involvement in the

Tibetan struggle which had began since 1955, and of its being instrumental in providing a base at Kalimpong, a commanding centre of Tibetan rebellion. There allegations were sharply refuted by the Prime Minister, who while reacting, strongly supported the Tibetan cause on humanitarian grounds. To quote him, "India's sympathy was based on sentiments and humanitarian reasons. Also on certain feeling of kinship with the Tibetan people derived from long-established religious and cultural contacts. It was an instinctive reaction."[14]

On the issue of Kalimpong as a centre for Tibetan rebels he added, these allegations were not justified. He said:

> ...we have a large number of people of Tibetan stock living in India as Indian nationals. We have also some Tibetan émigrés in India. All of these deeply respect the Dalai Lama. Some of these have been exceedingly unhappy at developments in Tibet; some no doubt have anti-Chinese sentiments."[15]

Thus he admitted that Kalimpong had been a centre for trouble and not a centre for commanding Tibetan rebels. Moreover, while responding to queries from the various members in Parliament, he categorically mentioned in the Lok Sabha on 27 April 1959 :

> Our broad policy was governed by three factors; (1) the preservation of the security and integrity of India; (2) Our desire to maintain friendly relations with China; and (3) Our deep sympathy for the people of Tibet. That policy we shall continue to follow, because we think that a correct policy, not only for the present but even more so for the future.[16]

To this complicated situation most of the leaders from almost all parties reacted sharply and asked the Government of India to extend a helping hand towards Tibet. To mention a few specifically, U.N. Dhebar said, "One can say to Tibetans who have been the victims of this unhappy episode that they have our deepest sympathies in their tour of trails."[17] Ashok Mehta, M.P. said, that the Dalai Lama must be allowed to function in India as the leader, spokesman and symbol of Tibetan people's struggle for independence. Defining India's interest in Tibet, Mr. Mehta said that people of Tibetan culture and origin lived on the Indian side of the Himalayas. "They are profoundly and deeply disturbed over developments in Tibet," he said, adding that India's interest in the freedom of Tibet was therefore deeper than in the freedom of colonial peoples in other parts of the world.[18] He added, "For India, Tibet was not only a question of moral obligation and cultural religious ties, our national security is involved.[19] He was even of the opinion that the Dalai Lama should be given complete freedom of action in India.[20] The Praja Socialist Party passed a resolution on Tibet, mentioning that "The executive is confident that Tibetans needing asylum would be welcome in India, our traditional hospitality and friendliness being assured to them."[21] Mrs. Sucheta Kripalani said, "the Tibetan issue was a question of human right. The people of India could never reconcile themselves to the suppression of human rights."[22] It was the first time that the issue of Tibetan refugees had been discussed from the violation of human rights point of view.

At this juncture it is important to quote Nehru in the Rajya Sabha, on 4 May 1959:

> ...we should allow these refugees to earn their own living and give them freedom to do many things. Broadly speaking, of course we intend that we are not going to keep them as prisoners in camps... to some extent we are responsible when these people are coming in. we cannot let them loose on India... We have exercised our undoubted right to give asylum. I have said that Dalai Lama is perfectly a free agent to go where he likes in India to go back to Tibet.[23]

As a result, the Government of India allowed another large batch of Tibetan refugees, especially women and children into Bombdilla on 20 May 1959. Responding to this help offered by the Government of India and its people, at his first press conference in India on 20 June 1959 at Mussoorie, the Dalai Lama said:

> I and my people owe a great debt of gratitude for all that you have done to assist us in our struggle for survival and freedom. Your sympathy and support has given us courage and

strengthened our determination. I am confident and hope that you will contribute to lend the weight of our influence to the cause of peace and freedom for which the people of Tibet are fighting today.[24]

Indian Assistance in Rehabilitation

Once the refugees were in asylum in India they were in need of some immediate relief to live. At first, the Dalai Lama wanted all his people should be settled together in large concentrations close to the Tibetan frontier[25] but for obvious security reasons the Indian government refused to do it. Instead, to accommodate and help the Tibetan refugees particularly those who were coming through NEFA, and Bhutan, the Government of India with the assistance of the state governments of Assam and West Bengal had set up various transit camps at Missamari (Assam) and at Buxa somewhere in Cooch-Behar (West Bengal), where the welfare of the refugees was looked after by an Indian Officer until such time as the refugees could be moved to more permanent resettlement areas in different parts of India.

The camp at Buxa was a former British detention camp for political prisoners and was now used exclusively for the Tibetan clergy. At one time there were as many as 1,500 monks there, despite the situation at Buxa was bad. The camp at Missamari was little better. According to a Tibetan-speaking scholar, half the Tibetans died from the climate and neglect in the first year. A Swiss refugee group put the population of Missamari at upwards of 8,000 in 1960.[26]

In the camps they were given free rations, clothing and cooking utensils, plus medical facilities. Despite this assistance, many Tibetan refugees died in the camp due to the sudden change of climate and their arduous journey across the Himalayas. For instance by 1969, 200 monks had contracted tuberculosis, 80 of whom died. The 900 monks who were still there in 1969-70 were finally moved south to the Tibetan settlements at *Bylakuppe* and *Mundgod*. To overcome this critical situation, the Dalai Lama approached the Ministry of External Affairs of the Government of India, which was assigned the work pertaining to the relief and rehabilitation of Tibetan refugees with a request to resettle these people in cooler places where they might be temporarily employed.[27] Responding immediately, the Government of India agreed to send these refugees to various places such as Himachal Pradesh, Jammu and Kashmir, Kalimpong, Darjeeling, Arunachal Pradesh, Sikkim and Dehradun,and Mussoorie, all hilly areas where most of them were then employed as road labourers. It was a first attempt by the GOI to provide a means for economic independence to the refugees. It had established 95 road construction camps along the northern borderlands in India. These were areas in which the Tibetans were uniquely qualified to labour because of their physique. Despite massive aid from the Indian government and outside sources, these road building camps did not provide a source of livelihood for the Tibetan refugees as roadwork was irregular. Approximately 18,000 to 21,000 Tibetans were employed in road building, at an average wage of US$0.30 a day.[28] The conditions were so bad that Tibetan refugee officials admitted in 1964 that these workers were worse off than they would have been if they had remained in Tibet. The squalor, low pay, constant threat of illness, and the shortened life expectancy were not all the refugees had to endure.[29] The worst injustice was the separation of the children from their families due to irregular work and road labourers had to move from place to place where work was available, with their children and belongings. Therefore the GOI had taken the decision to keep away around five thousand children from their parents and send them to live in permanent refugee camps. Three thousand others were permitted to stay with their parents in the road camps, but only on the condition that those under fifteen would not be allowed to work.[30] Nevertheless, as is so often the case, a few extra pennies are always required; and there were frequent reports of children under the age of fifteen engaged in hazardous work.[31]

In view of this practical difficulty, the Dalai Lama made another request to Pandit Nehru, for rehabilitation of these refugees in some other parts of India. Thus to rehabilitate these refugees, the GOI had followed a strategy of creating a series of permanent agricultural settlements throughout India as agriculture seemed to be the most suitable occupation for them to follow in exile, particularly as almost all them were unfamiliar with modern industrial technology. The logic behind this was to resettle Tibetans then living in transit camps or working on road repairing teams and provide them assistance and resources so that within a period of five years they could become economically self-sufficient thus reducing India's economic burden. The other point is with the help of such agriculture settlements the Indian Government thought it would also help India's food needs by bringing unused land under cultivation.

So Pandit Nehru wrote to the Chief Ministers of State Governments asking them if there was land available in their territories for the resettlement of the Tibetan refugees and received a positive reply from the Mysore government.[32] As a result, an area of over 3000 acres of land for an initial group of 3,000 refugees, situated at Bylakuppe in Karnataka was leased for 99 years to the Tibetan refugees by Shri Nijlingappa the Chief Minister of Mysore Government. Thus, to rehabilitate the mass exodus of Tibetans, in December 1960, the first group of Tibetan refugees was sent from the various transit camps located in Himachal Pradesh, Arunachal Pradesh, Kalimpong and Sikkim to Mysore and adjacent areas of Karnataka, known as Mundgod in the Belgaum division. The same method was adopted by the Government of India in other parts of the country to rehabilitate these refugees, particularly at Chandragiri in Orissa, Manipet in Madhya Pradesh, Dehradun and Mussoorie in UP., etc.

Life in Settlement Camps

Tibetan refugees have been rehabilitated in Settlement Camps mainly in three sectors; firstly agriculture, secondly, agro-based industries and thirdly carpet-weaving and handicrafts. This will be discussed in detail in the following paragraphs.

According to T. Samphel,[33] the Secretary of DIIR,

> The Settlement camps are managed and controlled by various different authorities namely, the Tibetan Authority, Central Government of India, State Government of respective settlement and the District Collector. It is very important that the authority takes the responsibility of these refugees.
>
> Whereas the scattered Camps are a spontaneous gathering at one place; secondly they do not get any government sanction; thirdly, nobody is responsible for any thing happens; fourthly, these refugees do not have consent from the local people; and lastly they do not get any economic opportunities by the Government.

The refugees who are living in scattered camps they are very much involved in street-marketing, selling wollen sweaters, seasonal goods, running small petty shops and restaurants.

Agriculture

In India there are total 17 agricultural settlements, out which in Karnataka State, alone, there are six such settlement, housing over 200,000 people. Apart from these there are also settlements in other parts of India,), three in Arunachal Pradesh, at Tezu Miao and Bomdila and in Ladakh there are two settlements, and each at Orissa (Chandgiri), Madhya Pradesh (Manipet), Maharashtra (Bhandara), Uttar Pradesh (Herbertpur), Sikkim (Rawangla) and in West Bengal (Darjeeling). The first of the rehabilitation agriculture settlements was located in the state of Mysore on forest land which had in the past sustained agriculture. This settlement, the first of its kind in India, is called Mundakuppe. The Government of India also provided accommodation along with the basic infrastructure necessary for daily survival. Facilities had been provided to these refugees to enable them to supplement their income by working in poultry-farming piggeries and dairies.[34] This was the most advanced settlement, largely because it received much technical assistance from abroad and from official organizations in India. This aid has included the establishment of a dairy farm by the National

Christian Council of India, the sending of agricultural experts and trucks by the Swiss, founding a carpet-weaving centre and setting up a work centre for the elderly by the AECTR.[35] Today the settlement houses numbers over 20,000 to 25,000 and some have become so well off that it has become more usual for young, impoverished Indian boys to be taken in by Tibetan families and also to help the poor farmers of the local areas for seeds, irrigation facilities and exchanging the farm equipments for better yield. In return for room and board these Indians would do a variety of household tasks such as hauling drinking water from the wells or just manual work in the farm in the absence of the Tibetan refugees. Presently most of the refugees are out for trading in various cities relying on local people's efforts in agriculture during the off seasons.[36]

The first five years were so prosperous that bicycles, horses and gambling began to proliferate, while Tibetans were increasingly able to hire landless Indians for labour needed in their fields. Around 80 per cent of the Tibetan refugees in south India living on the income of the agriculture settlements and overall 50 percent of refugees are belong to the agricultural settlements, most of which located in south and central India, viz., Karnataka, Maharashtra, and Madhya Pradesh.[37] These refugees were given on an average one acre of land each by the Government of India. Moreover they received agriculture equipment like bullocks, tractors, agricultural implements, seeds and fertilizers and other tools of trade. The farmers used to grow various cash crops suited to the local climate, but maize has proven to be the most productive and economically viable product in most of the places. Tibetans worked very hard on these several hectares of virgin and barren land converting it into cultivable land. Each agricultural settlement now has a co-operative society to help the settlers market their goods outside the refugee enclaves. In these settlements, the crops grown are mainly maize, wheat, paddy, potatoes and also important crops like ragi, soya beans, mustard and barley. For instance, the hard work of Tibetan refugees in Karnataka in the agricultural sector was appreciated by the Government of India as well as by the Karnataka State Government, since they had brought almost 25000 acres of barren land under irrigation.[38]

In contrast, the settlement at Manipet in Madhya Pradesh State is in a very poor condition. Established in 1963, through a Government of India grant of 2,132,200 rupees (roughly US$300,000), it had as many as 5,000 inhabitants at one time.[39] Moreover the resettlement policy in the north-east frontier at Arunachal Pradesh was literally frustrating due to harshness of the climate, the poverty of soil and the inacessibility of the chosen locations. The two thousand settlers at Changlang, found that their efforts to establish themselves were frustrated since there was an absence of sufficient capital for the provision of machinery, fertilizers and seeds, so these remote settlers have proved a failure.[40] The major differences between the settlement at Manipet and that at Bylakuppe were the land conditions and the degree of outside technical assistance. The camp at Manipet is in a dense forest, in constant danger from tigers, snakes and adverse weather conditions — all of which have taken a heavy toll in lives. Help for the community came largely in the form of funds from the AECTR. A hospital was built in 1964, only to be suddenly and mysteriously closed down three years later. The YMCA also sent a volunteer teacher. However, by 1978 there were only 1,100 inhabitants left at Manipet; and they were living without electricity, industry, or irrigation. Morale was very low, and there was little to show for fifteen years of labour.[41]

Whereas the situation in Karnataka at Bylakupee, (in Bylakupee there are three agriculture settlements which are over-crowded by around 100,000 refugees), may be envied by Tibetans living in other agricultural settlement Kollegal, Mundgod, and Hunsur agriculture settlements.[42] In these settlements it was found that after forty years, the water and electricity facilities were not very satisfactory, there were no approach roads in the settlements electricity is not there, most of the time it is something like load-shedding and the hospital was inadequate.[43] The available education was so poor that only rich families were sending their children to schools in

Bangalore, while those who were unable to afford such an expense, but were equally concern about their children's education, were keeping them at home rather than sending them to the Tibetan schools. There is also the problem of a shortage of land. Way back in the 1960s, each refugee received one acre of land. However, population increases due to either through immigration or birth, the average plot of land is now approximately half an acre per person.[44] Still it is very difficult to sustain the life in the settlements with fixed land size and the continuously increasing members of the family with scarcity of water and electricity. The greater difficulty is with self–funding the problem of how many years can one survive only on agriculture with low yield and minimum resources. Nevertheless, after forty years of technological and financial assistance, whatever it might be, the settlements representatives due to various reasons could not achieve establishing even the most rudimentary social welfare scheme for the needy.

In these settlements the day-to-day administration is run by an official appointed by the Dalai Lama; this person known as the Representative. This Representative is in many respects considered as the Chief of the settlement. He can virtually command people within the settlement as whole sole authority. One could observe that upon studying the administrative structure, the present system put an end to the traditional Tibetan serf - lord relationship.

Agro-based industry

However, the scarcity of land for agriculture particularly in northern India, and the lack of aptitude for agriculture among the young Tibetans, led the Government of India and representatives of the Dalai Lama to accommodate the rest of Tibetan refugees in other sectors such as agro-based industries.[45] Thus, the Government of India started eight industrial projects for them; to co-ordinate these projects, The Tibetan Industrial Rehabilitation Society was set up in 1965. The basic aim of this society was to implement employment-oriented programmes such as setting up woollen mills, and of tea estates which could provide employment as well as rehabilitation to the Tibetan refugees. Moreover, the society had a programme for rehabilitating refugees in industries such as lime-stone quarries, hydrated lime plants and fibre-glass factories in Himachal Pradesh and Uttar Pradesh. Unfortunately, some of these industries failed largely due to lack of technical knowledge, poor management and limited funding.[46] Tibetan society has now changed its emphasis to agricultural development, despite the difficulties of the terrain, and to the profitable occupation of handicrafts such as hand-woven carpets, shoulder bags and costume jewelry for which ready markets are available and accessible.[47] The Himalayan Marketing Association in Delhi has now been established to facilitate this cottage industry as a useful additional source of income to Tibetan families. Nevertheless, over the years, the situation has changed gradually and the refugees have now adapted to being an industrial and business management community. But, as a result of early experience, special efforts were made at various levels especially, voluntary training courses were offered to them in various trades, social welfare, nursing and so on.[48]

Carpet-weaving and Handicrafts

As a part of these rehabilitation programmes, along with agriculture and agro-based industries, the third sector i.e., carpet-weaving and handicrafts in which a maximum number of Tibetan refugees have been rehabilitated, has proved to be the most successful industrial enterprise in comparison with the other two sectors. Especially, as carpet-weaving is the century-old tradition of Tibetans, many of the settlements still concentrate on the production of carpets and handicrafts and have prospered economically. Handicrafts and carpet-weaving centres have been set up at Bylakuppe, Chandragiri, Manipet, Dalhousie, Darjeeling and Kalimpong, where more than 5000 Tibetan refugees are now working. It is important to note that since Tibetan carpets are beautiful and of high quality they are mostly exported to foreign, especially European countries. This helps not only the Tibetans to earn income, but also earns a significant amount of foreign exchange for India. At present, in this sector, more than ten per cent of the work force is involved, this being particularly true of the women and children who do not go on to higher education. The significance of this industry to the Tibetans is that it keeps traditional Tibetan crafts alive and creates greater awareness in the rest of the world about Tibet and its people. Apart from carpet-weaving, Tibetans are trained in weaving textiles and producing clothes, wood-carving, painting and metal-work. In some places, along with carpet-weaving the Tibetans sell other traditional Tibetan articles such as distinctively ethnic woollen clothes, religious icons, etc. In addition, tailoring fashionable garments for tourists has also emerged as an income strategy. To preserve this rich Tibetan cultural heritage and to look after the handicraft products and emporiums at various places throughout the world, the Department of Home of the Tibetan Government in Exile has set up Tibet House in New Delhi.[49]

Education

Education is another field in which Tibetans are known for their conscientiousness. To quote His Holiness the Dalai Lama:

> Our goal for now and the future should be to keep abreast with other people of the world in all aspects of educational progress and development. Therefore after coming to India as refugees, our primary initiative has been the education of our children, the future seeds of Tibet who will carry out our national task, be it political or spiritual.[50]

Education has been the top priority on the rehabilitation agenda, therefore almost each and every settlement of Tibetan refugees has education facilities for Tibetan children. The Department of Education, since its inception in 1960 is the apex body responsible for providing support for the educational and welfare needs of nearly 28,000 students in 71 schools in India.[51] Comprising both residential and day schools, these institutions range from the pre-primary to the senior secondary level. These schools emphasize the integration of Tibetan language, values and culture into the curriculum and extra-curricular activities. Approximately, 92% of all Tibetan children in exile between the age of six and seventeen go to school and 84% attend school.[52] It reveals the fact of a high literacy rate among Tibetans, and their desire for education not only to survive, but also to understand the world in a better manner; and enable them to face any challenge or threat to their existence. It energizes them to struggle in all walks of life even while in exile.

The first school for Tibetan children was established at Mussoouri in March 1960. Eventually the Indian Minister of Education formed the Central Tibetan Schools Administration (CTSA), and by 2000 the Ministry was operating 30 Residential schools monitored by the Central government as well as respective state governments. In addition to this, there is a total 45 schools which are directly run by the Department of Education, Tibetan Government-in-Exile.

Except for the teaching of Tibetan language and history – carried out by Tibetan teachers – Indian teachers were employed, using English as the medium of instruction. [In the light of this, the Tibetan refugee accusation that the Chinese are destroying Tibetan culture by using Chinese for teaching in the schools in Tibet, rather than Tibetan, is curious][53] According to an interview with the some of the literate officers in the Education department, however, most of the curriculum taught in the Tibetans schools is not up to the mark as they are unable to compete with the other local schools or colleges and develop the students ability and future vision.

Not all Tibetan children attend school. There are a few schools in the agricultural settlements and residential schools but the poor conditions, of course, do not allow them to continue their education. Moreover economic opportunities like street marketing and instant income to satisfy immediate needs attract them to leave schooling and earn money. One positive impact of this trend is that you see any young Tibetan not dependent on the mercy of either Tibetan funds or the Indian government's financial assistance.

Fresh Arrivals

As reported in a book by T. Palkashappa, after examining a group of refugees to determine their motives for having left Tibet, questioned 869 families in 1974-1975. He found that the Tibetans listed their reasons in the following order of descending importance.

1. Anxiety over not being allowed to remain practicing Buddhists;
2. Rumours of atrocities committed by the Han;
3. Rumours of Tibetans being prevented from marrying Tibetans
4. Rumours of Tibetans being compelled to marry Han;
5. The departure of the Dalai Lama; and
6. Incessant political meetings, insecurity over the future, and the educating of children to watch and report the behaviour of their parents. [54]

Judging from formal and informal interviews with many fresh arrivals in Dharamsala, during a field trip in May-June 1999, I observed that every month, hundreds of new refugees enter Indian borders. Some of them register with the reception centre some of them don't. The unregistered refugees join the scattered camps anywhere in India depending upon to whom they know in the area. The Secretary of Home Ministry of Tibetan Government-in-Exile Mr. Wangyal said, the ministry genuinely scrutinizes the fresh arrivals to find out who the refugees are and then admits them to the Tibetan Reception Centre. According to him there are four types of refugees who come regularly and seek an asylum in India. Those are:

1. Who fled from Tibet due to the Chinese Government's torture and atrocity
2. Monks and Nuns to take religious education about Buddhism in India as this is prevented in China.
3. The pilgrimage population which comes here just to get the blessings from the Dalai Lama and intends to return after that.
4. The youngsters who comes to India for the purpose of good moral education as they do not get the opportunity in China.

> In this case, parents of these children are instrumental in sending them out of fear that their future in China is bleak.[55]

After formal and routine processing, the Reception Centre allows them to take rest for a week and to naturalize with the weather conditions; then after an audience with the Dalai Lama, these refugees are sent to the Emergency Relief Centre, from there they are shifted to temporary shelters and the next stage is to move to transit camps. After spending a few months in these camps, the refugees are sent to the closest settlements according to their interest either in agriculture or handicrafts where they are educated and trained in specific fields of art, for their self sufficiency and daily livelihood. But the problem is that these facilities are no more available for newcomers as already these settlements are overcrowded as well as suffering from their own internal problems. So naturally the younger generations who are fresh arrivals from Tibet are generally reluctant to enter these settlements and prefer to live in isolated scattered camps. These camps are totally different in nature from the settlements.

Overall impression of the Tibetan refugees in their respective settlements is they do take the utmost care of infants and kids in baby nursing homes or crèches, while their parents are at work. However due to the pressure for self-sufficiency and heavy burden of expenses, in Tibetan society, the parents of a Tibetan child can take care of their child at least till the age of 16[56] and allow it to work on its own and be independent in almost all walks of life.

Interestingly, at the same time, it does not overlook or isolate the elderly Tibetans in exile as

> ...today they were the pioneers who first organized the settlements and the structure of the Central Tibetan Administration (CTA). It is they who remember Tibet before the invasion and brought with them the Tibetan culture, language, and the spirit of independence.[57]

Thus as recommended by the Dalai Lama, to allow these elderly people to devote the rest of their lives to religion and prayer, the Department of Home runs homes for elderly men and women, and the CTRC runs a project to find sponsors for needy and old people.[58] In this way, more than 12,000 elderly refugees are living all over in settlements spread across India. They are mostly concentrated at McLeod Ganj as their spiritual leader lives there in his palace and the monastery is close by. These elderly people always dream that in their lifetime if they could not go to their homeland to live or die, they can at least spend the rest of their lives under the shadow of their spiritual leader.

Another prominent feature that of Tibetan herbals and medicine, is a vital and inherent aspect of Tibetan society. It has significantly contributed to the host country as well as to the world. The Tibetan medical and Astro-Institute located in Lower McLeod Ganj, is an autonomous body often visited by many foreigners for cures and to further their medical research in this field. The Tibetan Medical Institute has 36 branch clinics in various parts of India and Nepal to promote Tibetan medical care to Tibetans and the local population

Before discussing the challenges in socio-economic adaptation one could see the work of Dawa Norbu, a Tibetan refugee himself, well educated and currently teaching at JNU, New Delhi. This reputed scholar on Tibet, in his two important articles namely *Tibetan Refugees in South Asia: A Case of Peaceful Adjustment*, (1996)[59] and secondly, *Refugees from Tibet: Structural Causes of Successful Settlements*, (2001)[60]. In both articles, Norbu has highlighted the trauma faced by Tibetans after arrival in India and the successful settlement subsequently. He has discussed the tension between the refugees and host population especially the elite of the Indian society as well as the security implications of their presence in India and South Asia. In another article he has given credit of for successful resettlement to Indian leadership and to some political decisions of the GOI. He has also admired the Tibetan government-in Exile and various NGOs which are active in supporting the Tibetan cause. Apart from this one point in which he repeatedly mentions about Tibetan refugees, is self-governance. This could be a guiding spirit for the refugees in rest of the world.

Foreign Assistance

Apart from the treasury of Dalai Lamas the bulk of the funds come, from the centre and state governments of India, which provides land, food rations, medical assistance, and more general relief aid. The total amount spent on the refugees will probably never be calculated, although we know the Indians had spent over US$6,000,000 by 1962.[61] In the early years the slack was taken up by foreign governments and private relief agencies; however, as these became less involved, the Indian government became more involved. By the end of 1965 US$2,625,000 had been spent on the agricultural settlements; 750,000 rupees (roughly US$110,000) was spent solely on the Bylakuppe Settlement in southern India at a time when its population number 3,000.[62]

After the Indian government, the major sources of funds were Western nations – through both governmental and private channels. In the early years (1959 – 62) organizations such as CARE, the International Red Cross, the YMCA, Catholic Relief, Church World Service, the International Rescue Committee, and Save the Children Fund all participated.[63] In addition, Swiss and American governments and, later on, the United Nations High Commissioner for Refugees (1964–73) also contributed to refugee assistance. During the first decade of exile, the Tibetan refugees received US$5,300,000 in direct aid from the American government. One estimate of the total amount provided ran to more than US$20,000,0000; this would average over US$400 received for every man, woman and child.[64]

In the process of building self-sustaining and viable settlements, the contributions of foreign voluntary agencies have been of enormous help. According to an American researcher, John S. Conway,

> Beginning in 1966 with the provision of 3,500,000 US dallars from the funds of the European Rufugee Campaign, large-scale

> rehabilitation projects have been organized and financed mainly from European and North American sources. The Board of Trustees for the Common Project of the European Rufugee Campaign established, as its Indian Partner, The Mysore Resettlement and Development Agency (MYRDA) which has been responsible for the creation of four major settlements in Karnataka...[65]

Moreover there were private funds collected through the various friendship societies like The Tibetan Friendship Group formed in the United States — followed closely by similar groups in France, Switzerland, England, Norway, South Africa, Australia and New Zealand as well as the Indo-Tibet friendship society. These groups raised and donated funds and encouraged the financial adoption of individual refugees by their members.

In the United States, the American Emergency Committee for Tibetan Refugees (AECTR) was hastily formed in March 1959. Under the leadership of journalist Lowell Thomas and Supreme Court Justice William O. Douglas, this agency was to remain in existence only a few months, in order to help the Tibetans get settled in exile.[66] Although the complete story of the committee is yet untold, there remains much speculation and considerable circumstantial evidence that a major source of its funding was the CIA. While the AECTR's literature attributes its genesis to the efforts of Magnus I. Gregerson of the Columbia University's College of Physicians and Surgeons, other documents attribute it to the efforts of one Marvin Liebman, the secretary to the anti-communist *Committee of One Million against the Admission of Communist China to the United Nations*. Liebman was a prominent rightist, anticommunist crusader, who within two weeks of the fighting in Lhasa in March 1959, had consulted with the US Department of State's Public Affairs Adviser of the Bureau of Far Eastern Affairs, and the AECTR was born.[67] By December that year it was able to send US$200,000 and medical supplies to refugees in India. By 1961 it had provided a total of US$707,503 in cash and supplies.[68]

In this way we can see how the Tibetan refugees are settled and rehabilitated by the GOI and the Tibetan administration with the help of foreign aid agencies mainly the International Red Cross Society, and individual donor countries especially from Europe. Recently countries like Japan and Israel have involved themselves in the rehabilitation work of Tibetan refugees in India. Also due to the attraction of Buddhism and the spiritual nature of the Dalai Lama, many individuals visit Dharamsala and render their services to those who are in need

Indo-Tibetan Border Police (ITBP) Force

The Indo-Tibetan Border Police Force was conceived on 24 October1962 for the protection of India's frontiers along the Indo-Tibetan Border covering 2115 kms from Karakoram Pass to Lipulekh Pas and the tri-junction of India, Nepal and China. Incredible though it may sound, only four battalions were sanctioned to begin with, to fill up the security vacuum that was prevalent at that time on the Indo- Tibet border.[69] Most of these recruits were from among Tibetan refugees. It was a planned strategy to rehabilitate the refugees. The logic behind this could be that these refugees were more familiar and known to this mountainous region of the Himalayas and had experience of fighting with Chinese army when they were in Tibet. Apart from this, the forward post of Indian border is located at altitudes ranging from 9000 to 18000 feet. Most of the forward posts remain cut off and cannot use the surface route during the winter months. The border posts are exposed to the fury and violence of nature such as snow blizzards, avalanches, and landslides. In these circumstance only the ITBP protects the Indian frontiers against any possible Chinese threat to India's integrity and sovereignty. Later in view of the additional responsibilities and the task redefined in 1976, the Force was restructured in 1978. ITBP was initially raised under the CRPF (Central reserve Police Force) Act; however in 1992, Parliament enacted the ITBP Act, and rules thereunder were framed in 1994.[70] Although at the beginning the ITBP jawans were mainly from the Tibetan community, recently the government has allowed recruiting even non-Tibetans in the Force. The main task of the ITBP force is to keep vigil on the northern borders, detection and prevention of border violation, and promotion of a sense of security in the local populace.

References

1. Chanakya Sen, *Tibet Disappears,* (Bombay: Asia Publishing House, 1960), p.26
2. Tsering Shakya, *The Dragon in the Land of Snows: A History of Modern Tibet Since 1947,* (London : Pimlico, 1999) p.213
3. Chanakya Sen, p.26
4. Nehru's Statement in the Lok Sabha on March 23, 1959, as reproduced in Chanakya Sen, n.1, p.162
5. Ibid.,
6. Quoted in Tsering Shakya, n.2, p.213
7. Ibid., pp.213-214
8. Nehru's Statement in the Lok Sabha on 30 March 1959, as reproduced in *Dalai Lama and India: Indian Public and Prime Minister on the Tibetan Crisis,* (New Delhi : The Institute of National Affairs, 1959), pp.78-79
9. *The Indian Nation,* 3 April 1959, as reproduced in Ibid., pp38-39
10. Noel Barber, *The Flight of the Dalai Lama,* (London : Hodder and Stoughton, 1960), pp.118-119
11. Tsering Shakya writes that the Tibetan had asked the Americans to approach the GOI for asylum. This was a serious misjudgment on the part of the Tibetans and Americans. For details see his book, *The Dragon in the Land of Snows: A History of Modern Tibet Since 1947,* (London : Pimlico, 1999) p.215
12. Melinda Liu, *When Heaven Shed Blood,* in *Newsweek,* (New York), vol.xxxxiii, No. 16, April 19, 1999. pp.38-39
13. *Nehru's Statement in the Lok Sabha* on 27 April 1959, n. 8, pp.118-119
14. Ibid.
15. Ibid.
16. Ibid., pp.143-144

17. Ibid., p.144
18. Ibid.
19. Ibid., p. 47
20. Ibid., p.151
21. Ibid.
22. Ibid., p.152
23. *Nehru's Statement in Rajya Sabha*, on 4 May 1959, as reproduced in Chanakya Sen, n. 1, pp.217-234
24. Dalai Lama's Statement on 20 June 1959, Ibid., p. 158
25. A. Tom Grunfeld, *The Making of Modern Tibet*, (Bombay: Oxford University Press, 1987), p.191
26. Ibid.,
27. *Tibetans in Exile 1959-69*, (Dharamsala: CTRC Publication, 1969), p.3
28. A. Tom Grunfeld, n. 25, p.190
29. Ibid.
30. Ibid.
31. Ibid.,193
32. *Tibetans in Exile 1959-69*, n.27, pp.4-5
33. It was told by Mr. T. Samphel, the Secretary of Department of Information and International Relations, Tibetan Government-in-Exile in and interview conducted during the field trip at Dharamsala in May-June 1999.
34. B.N.Banerjee, *India's Assistance to the Tibetan Refugees since 1959, Tibetan Bulletin*, (Dharamsala), March- April 1982, p.16
35. A.T. Grunfeld, n. 25, pp.192-193
36. This opinion is based on the field trip conducted in these five settlement camps in Karnataka during May-June 2002
37. Ibid.,
38. *Life in Exile*, (Dharamsala: Deptt. of Home, CTRC Publication, 1992) p. 11
39. A.T. Grunfeld, n. 25, pp. 192-193
40. John S. Conway, *The Tibetan Community in Exile, Pacific Affairs*, (Canada), Vol. 48, No.1, Spring 1975, p.78
41. A.T. Grunfeld, n. 25, p 194
42. Interviews in these agriculture camps during May-June 2002
43. Ibid.

44. As it was told by the Chief Representative who sits in Bangalore and controls of these six agriculture settlement camps located in Karnataka in an interview 31 May 2002
45. *Life in Exile*, n. 38, p. 9
46. Ibid.
47. John S. Conway, n.40, p. 81
48. Life in Exile, n. 38, p.10
49. Ibid.
50. *Education in Exile : Building Our Future through Education*, (Dharamsala: DOE Publications, 1998) p.5
51. Ibid., p.4
52. Life in Exile, n. 38, p.12
53. A.T. Grunfeld, n. 25, pp. 189-190
54. T.C. Palakshappa, *Tibetans in India: A Case Study of Mundgod Tibetans*, (New Delhi : Sterling Publishers, 1978),
55. Field trip to Karnataka during May-June 2002
56. Ibid.
57. Life in Exile, n. 38, p. 15
58. Ibid., p. 16
59. Dawa Norbu, *Tibetan Refugees in South Asia: A Case of Peaceful Adjustment*, in Muni and Baral, *Refugees and Regional Security in South Asia*,(New Delhi : RCSS and Konark, 1996) pp. 78-98
60. -----------------, *Refugees from Tibet : Structural Causes of Successful Settlements*, in S. K. Roy,(ed.), *Refugees and Human Rights*, (New Delhi : Rawat, 2001). pp.199-235
61. A.T. Grunfeld, n. 25, pp.189-190
62. Ibid.
63. Ibid.
64. Ibid.
65. John S. Conway, n.40, pp.78-79
66. A.T. Grunfeld, n. 25, pp.189-190
67. Ibid.
68. Ibid.
69. For details, see website of ITBP, *www.itbp.html*
70. Ibid.

4

Reconstruction of Tibet in Exile

Being aware of suppression of Tibetan ethnic identity and culture by the Chinese in China, and of the uncertainty of the fate of Tibetan refugees in the neighbouring countries, the Dalai Lama decided to rehabilitate the refugees first and made extra efforts to protect its unique culture. As a part of this policy decision the Dalai Lama formed few organizations with the help of some prominent Indian leaders and sympathizers to the Tibetan cause. The main task was how to reconstruct Tibet as a nation, obviously without territory or sovereignty but based purely on nationalism, and at the same time maintaining its separate identity and protecting its culture, its spiritual and political traditions especially when its people were refugees in a third country. However this task was assigned to the Central Tibetan Relief Committee (CTRC) originally known as Central Relief Committee (CRC) and the Tibetan Government in Exile and the various religious and cultural institutions. And these institutions are doing their job sincerely with dedication at least till today.

Role of Central Tibetan Relief Committee (CTRC)

The Central Tibetan Relief Committee (CTRC) originally known as Central Relief Committee (CRC), is an organization started in 1959 by some prominent Indians like J. B. Kriplani as its chairperson, to co-ordinate relief assistance between the Government of India and representatives of the Dalai Lama for the rehabilitation of Tibetan refugees. The main objective of the CTRC is to help the poor, needy, backward and under-privileged within the Tibetan Community in exile. It has been consistently instrumental in obtaining assistance from foreign aid agencies not only in the agricultural sector but also in the form of food, medicine, etc., and sometimes even cash. It has also planned Handicraft Projects aiming at generating employment for the more under-privileged sections of the community, unsettled refugees and school drop-outs. At the same time, it is trying to diversify and encourage the production of more varied crafts, tailoring, knitting, embroidery and wood-carving, in its attempts to organize the training programmes to increase employment prospects. In this way, the CTRC plays a very significant role in rehabilitating the Tibetan refugees in exile all over South Asia. It works as the heart and soul of the development programmes planned for Tibetan refugees. According to one of the publications of the Tibetan Government-in-Exile, the CTRC helps those Tibetans who are in need in the following manner:

- Runs, and assists with development programmes to help the poor, needy, and underprivileged;
- Co-ordinates the efforts of the Government of India, relief agencies and individuals and their mobilizes their resources;
- Plans and carries out the resettlement and rehabilitation of Tibetan refugees;
- Promotes the handicraft industry through centres and other self-help co-operative ventures;
- Promote agricultural projects to increase food production;
- Assists industrial and vocational training in craft schools and other training centres;
- Assists emergency relief work for victims of natural disasters;
- Receives and distributes donations, such as food, medicine, clothing and equipment;

- Runs educational and orientation courses to help the resettlement of refugees.[1]

Tibetan Government in Exile

Soon after his arrival in India, the Dalai Lama successfully negotiated the establishment of the Tibetan Government-in-Exile with the Indian authorities.[2] Within a month, on 29 April 1959, he reestablished the Tibetan Government-in-Exile at Musoorie, named as the Central Tibetan Administration (CTA) of His Holiness Dalai Lama.[3] Basically it is the continuation of the Government of Independent Tibet. In May 1960, the exile Government was moved to McLeod Ganj at Dharamsala in Himachal Pradesh. The CTA is reorganized as the Tibetans sole and legitimate government and has set itself the twin task of rehabilitating Tibetan refugees and restoring the freedom of Tibet.[4] On 2 September 1960, the Tibetan Parliament-in- Exile came into existence, later on renamed as Assembly of Tibetan People's Deputies. Moreover, this arrangement proved to be of the utmost importance for Tibetans in exile to monitor and handle its cultural and political affairs through the Central Tibetan Administration (CTA) which works as an organizational link between the Indian Government, Western aid organizations and the exiled Tibetan community spread all over the world. This does not mean that the GOI and the state governments had no objection to giving the DLG *defacto* internal administrative control over the refugees living in the camps or outside the camps.[5] Moreover, the Government of India does not recognize any formal legal or political status of government-in-exile[6] due to political reasons, particularly after the Sino-India war of 1962. In a similar manner the GOI also refused to resettle all Tibetans in one area in north India as the DLG (the Dalai Lama Government) suggested.[7] The important point here is despite all these considerations and compulsions the GOI took a fundamental decision, which was to rehabilitate the refugees.

On 10 March 1963, the Tibetan Constitution was promulgated by the Dalai Lama. It was an attempt to integrate modern Western concepts of parliamentary democracy with the feudal traditions of Tibet[8] and according to whose principles the present administration is run.[9] It begins with a classic understatement: whereas it has become increasingly evident that the system of government which has hitherto prevailed in Tibet has not proved sufficiently responsive to the present needs and future development of the people and proceeds to guarantee equality before the law, due process of law, right to legal counsel, freedom of speech, assembly, travel, association and residence in Tibet.[10] The actual work on the Constitution was started in 1960 under the Information and Publicity Office and drafted with the help of an Indian lawyer. By 1961 the main outlines of the Constitution had been written bearing very strongly the imprint of the Dalai Lama's ideas in this regard. This draft outline was sent to all Tibetans in India and in other countries in a sort of referendum and the answer came back in an overwhelming support for the idea of such a constitution.[11] According to A. Tom Grunfeld, "Interestingly, for a constitution based on Buddhist ideology, there is no stipulation banning 'unclean castes' [butchers, tanners, and corpse-handlers], a common practice in Tibet prior to 1959."[12] It shows that Tibetans wanted to retain the social inequality as one of its feudal characteristics in the Tibetan society.

At this juncture it is also important to note, Rinzin Thargyal, Osteras's comments in the article *Is There a Process of Secularization Among the Tibetans in Exile?* :

> Theoretically, social inequality is incompatible with Buddhism since its philosophy is based on the doctrine of universal Buddha nature and pan-human consanguinity. Honouring pan-human consanguinity is antithetical to the concept of inequality, human bondage and inhumanity. Tibet can exemplify a case in point. Despite Buddhism's injunction to practise democracy, the erstwhile Tibetan polity had not been pervaded by democratic traditions in comparison with the monastic community in Tibet. One reason may be that very few farsighted leaders had the opportunity to implement reforms whereas many myopic politicians squandered their time and energy by indulging in political rivalries and intrigue.[13]

On the other hand, it also decided to experiment with modern democracy in preparation for a future Tibet. One can find certain changes, of which a few are:

> Instead of hereditary rights, as in the old Tibetan Theocracy, merit and education were the main criteria for the selection of Tibetan youth as the officials of the administration. The administration is headed by a cabinet of appointed ministers dealing with the old and new concerns of the Tibetan people; an assembly of elected representatives of the exiled community standing for the three major regions of Tibet (U-Tsang, Amdo and Kham) and the five religious orders; a working committee for detained policies; and for the settlements, local self-government, each linked conceptually to its antecedents in the homeland.[14]

In other words, there is no need of revolution to make the Tibetan system adapt to the conditions of the modern world. Thus at the beginning of their tenure in exile, the main concern of the Dalai Lama and his administration was the rehabilitation of thousands of Tibetan refugees. To do so, the rehabilitation strategy which was agreed upon by the Tibetan administration, the Government of India and the aid organizations, concerned, called for the creation of permanent agricultural settlements throughout India. This was proved to be right by the Tibetan refugees by their extra-ordinary efforts, dedication and honesty to the cause.

The *Kashag*, cabinet, is the highest executive body of the Tibetan administration and its members, the *Kalons*, are directly appointed by the Dalai Lama. Each of *Kalons* heads one or two departments. The *Kashag* as a body supervises the entire administration. All important policies are discussed and decided in the meetings of National Working Committee which is held regularly once a month and it is chaired by the chairman of the Assembly.[15] Decisions are made by the elected representatives by majority vote.

The Tibetan Government-in-Exile has various departments, especially, the Home Information and International Relations, Education, Finance, Religious and

Cultural Affairs, Planning and Agriculture. The Department of Home is responsible for the rehabilitation and welfare of all Tibetan refugees in India, Nepal and Bhutan. It administers the Tibetan settlement camps, handicrafts centre and road construction camps, and it is also responsible for coordinating the various settlement camps in India and abroad. Moreover it also maintains contacts with variety of Indian and foreign aid agencies.[16] The department of Education is charged with the responsibility of working out a system that would combine the best of modern education with that of traditional culture, so that, children educated under this system would retain their traditional values and at the same time possess a modern, cosmopolitan outlook of life.[17] The department of Religious and Cultural Affairs, supervises the running of a number of monasteries and the education of young monks. The department maintains close contact with other Tibetan Buddhist centres all over the world and is a member of a number of International Buddhists committees. It also maintains two Buddhists Institutions of Higher Tibetan Studies located at Sarnath and Dharamsala.[18] The purpose of these two institutes is to produce highly educated Tibetan monks who are at the same time conversant with the main intellectual trends of the contemporary world.[19] The Finance department was established for the purpose of creating sufficient financial means for the Tibetan administration to be self-supporting.[20] The function of DIIR is to keep the outside world informed of the situation in Tibet and activities of the Tibetans in Exile. It also acts as Protocol Officer for the administration. It provides information to those who are interested in Tibetan affairs, issues press statements on important matters requiring the reactions of the administration and publishes periodicals and books in Tibetan and English.[21]

However, the Tibetan Government- in-Exile funds and finds itself in the unenviable position of having no 'legal' or 'constitutional' status with respect to Indian Law and consequently is not able to use coercive force to compel acquiescence with their policies. Hence, their continued operation as a 'government' depends completely on the voluntary compliance of the refugees, which, in turn, depends on the refugees' perceived self-interests and on their belief in the legitimacy of the DLG[22] (Dalai Lama's Government).

Realizing opposition and resentment among the young generation as well as certain sect of the Tibetan refugees,[23] about the traditional way of Tibetan life in the twenty-first century, in the 1990s, the Dalai Lama announced further democratization by which the composition of the National Assembly was increased to 46 members. Assembly was empowered to elect the Tibetan *Kashag* or the Council of Ministers, which was made answerable to it.

The democratization of the Tibetan Government-in-Exile has touched the milestone of one of its attributes of free democratic government when on 29 July 2001, millions of Tibetans across the world, polled to vote directly for the first time to choose their chief Kalon or Head of the Government-in-Exile, who will be only second to the Dalai Lama in popularity and reverence.[24] Professor Samdhang Rinpoche, former Director of the Central Institute of Higher Tibetan Studies at Sarnath, has been elected as the Head of the Tibetan cabinet and first Prime Minister of the Tibetan Government-in-Exile.[25] It is said that, this is an exercise to not only ensure people's participation in political affairs but will also make the political representative more accountable to the people.[26] This Deputy of the Dalai Lama, will be looked upon as a leader who will also steer the political struggle of the Tibetans, who still dream of returning to their home land.

To make a point here, after marching towards democracy, Tibetan Government-in-Exile does not allow the CTA to take power when Tibet becomes free.[27] The Dalai Lama states that the present exiled government would be dissolved as soon as Tibet is once again free.[28]

Thus the political reforms initiated by the Dalai Lama especially the democratic set-up of the exiled administration and government, created a good and positive impression of successful adaptation of Tibetans to India and its democratic system of government and led sympathy for it from the western world. It would also help to get greater amount of sponsorships from various foreign funding agencies and individual donors for the purpose of a variety of programmes and to keep Tibetan culture and separate identity alive.

Preservation of Tibetan Identity and Culture in Exile

The majority of Tibetan refugees who entered India in 1959 were nomads, monks, farmers and petty traders. According to one report published by Department of Information and International Relations (DIIR), during the 1991 election, the distribution of the Tibetan population in India follows as below: 70% of refugees belong to former *U-Tsang*, (Central Tibet), 25% from *Kham* (East Tibet), while only 5% from *Amdo*, (Northeast Tibet).[29] The refugees spoke only Tibetan with their own dialects which varies from region to region and had no inter-connection. Very few Tibetan families could understand either English or Hindi and these were mainly from aristocratic families or monks. As they were familiar with exclusively traditional political hierarchy and authority as well as involved in religion-bound culture and economic activities, the Tibetan refugees found it is very difficult to communicate and adjust to the existing socio-political system in India. Hence from the very beginning, the policies of the GOI were not intended to discourage or destroy Tibetan cultural institutions and traditions. Working along with the DLG and various foreign aid groups, the GOI launched a programme of rehabilitation within the framework compatible with the maintenance of Tibetan culture. Thus, the Dalai Lama, while in exile, has since the beginning, decided to accommodate the cultural component in establishing monasteries in almost each and every Tibetan settlement in India as well as abroad.

In anticipating the suppression of Tibetan culture and religious traditions in Tibet, the Dalai Lama, on one of the occasions of opening a school for Tibetan children, said,

> The children have been a special anxiety for me; there are over five thousand of them under sixteen. It is even harder for

> children than adults to be uprooted and taken suddenly to an entirely different environment, and many of them died, in the early days, from a change of food and climate. We had to do something drastic to preserve their health; and their education was also a matter of great importance. So, in the next generation, the five thousand children in India would become important, a nucleus to preserve the heritage of peaceful religion, tradition and culture.[30]

In exile, modern education was considered to be the very weapon to defend and preserve the religious and cultural heritage of Tibet, which in old Tibet was thought to be the undermining force of these aspects of Tibet's social and political structure. To enable themselves to be identified as Tibetan Buddhists better known as "nangpa" Tibetans in exile, the elite of religious figures, artists, writers, performers, academicians, musicians are particularly at the forefront for promotion and protection of the distinct culture and traditions of Tibetans. For instance, in Dharamsala, at Upper McLeod Ganj as well as in Lower McLeod Ganj, the buildings of the Tibetan Parliament in exile, Library of Tibetan Works and Archives are marked with detailed paintings of Tibetan art and architectural features. A separate institution has been set up to train young Tibetans in different fields of traditional culture, known as the Norbulingka Institute for Tibetan Culture at Sidhpura in Dharamsala. Basically this is just a replica of the Norbulingka Institute of Lhasa which was destroyed by the Chinese. Another institute, the Tibetan Institute of Performing Arts at Upper McLeod Ganj also looks after dances, and drama theatre of Tibetan tradition. There are many more such institutions situated mainly in Himachal Pradesh and Darjeeling, Kalimpong and Karnataka, to protect the culture of Tibetans in exile. The practice of religious and cultural traditions and ceremonies has largely been entrusted to those who were born in Tibet and known for their dedication to Tibet prior to their making the journey into exile. Moreover, the CTA has established a separate Department of Religious and Culture, which seeks to protect, preserve and promote Tibet's spiritual and cultural heritage.

In this way it has been proved that the true Tibetan culture is protected and preserved not just in Tibet, but in India as culturally Tibet and India have a century-old relationship. Girija Saklaini,[31] an Indian Sociologist, did some exhaustive study field work and research on Tibetan refugees living in Dharamsala, Delhi, and Deharadun (Northern India) and her findings are similarly positive like those of other researchers in India as well as abroad.

To mention here specifically, Melvyn Goldstein,[32] the American anthropologist who arrived at Bylakuppe in January 1966 to do field work, did a detailed study on Tibetan refugees particularly those who are settled in South India. The work mainly concentrates on the rehabilitation aspect of the refugees and discusses the cultural component which is an inherent part of Tibetan society. His argument is that Tibetan culture is very much protected by the GOI while rehabilitating the refugees. In the process while discussing the ethnic and political identity of Tibetan refugees, he argues, theoretically it is an attempt made by DLG and refugees to protect the sacred religious and cultural institutions and developing an important foundation for a nation-state.

> The introduction of Tibetans to modern education is important not only in the context of the continuing expansion of the mental horizon of the Tibetans in the outside world but also in the context of the larger process of the evolution of Tibetan society. The new education and the innate spirit of independence of the Tibetans are increasingly making the new generation of Tibetans aware of what is unique and special in their culture and what is important in the development of the modern world. It is this combination which is making the Tibetans asserts their sense of nationality and nationalism to more practical effect, signs of which are everywhere. If the Tibetan people hold fast to this orientation, no amount of modernisation will, in the long run, be in conflict with their nature and purpose.

References

1. *Tibetans in Exile 1959-69*, (Dharamsala : CTRC Publication, 1969), p.3

2. *Central Tibetan Administration: An Introduction*, (Dharamsala:Year N.A.) p.8
3. Ibid.,
4. A. Tom Grunfeld, *The Making of Modern Tibet*, (Bombay: Oxford University Press, 1987)
5. Melvyn C. Goldstein, *Tibetan Refugees in South India: A new Face to the Indo-Tibetan Interface, The Tibetan Society Bulletin*, Vol. 9, 1975, p.13
6. Ibid.
7. Ibid.
8. *Tibetans in Exile 1959-69*, n.1, p.311
9. Thubten Samphel, *A Culture in Exile; Tibetan Refugees in India, China Report*, (New Delhi), 24;3, 1998, p.239
10. Ibid.
11. *Tibetans in Exile*, n.1 p.312
12. A. Tom Grunfeld, n.4, p.
13. Rinzin Thargyal, Osteras, *Is There a Process of Secularization Among the Tibetans in Exile?*, (n.a.) p. 27
14. T. Samphel, n.9, pp.239-240
15. *Administrative leadership and Community Success* in *Tibet-84: 25 Years of Struggle and Reconstruction*, (Dhramsala: Organizing Committee, 1984), p. 29
16. Ibid.
17. Ibid, p.30
18. Ibid.
19. Ibid.
20. Ibid.
21. Ibid.
22. Melvyn Goldstein, n.5, p.20
23. Claiming to represent about 20,000 Tibetan refugees in India who are worshippers of *Dholgyal Shugden*- a Tibetan deity, accused the Dalai Lama led Tibetan Government-in-Exile of suppressing freedom of expression and right to worship. For details see, *The Hindu*, (New Delhi Edition) 12 November 2000
24. *Asian Age*, (Mumbai), 30 July 2001
25. *Times of India*, (Mumbai), 24 August 2001
26. *Asian Age*, n, 24
27. *Times of India*, n.25

28. Ibid.
29. Thomas Methfessel, Marburg, *Socioeconomic Adaptation of Tibetan refugees in South Asia over 35 years in Exile,* (n.a.) p.13
30. See, *My Land and my People, Memoirs of the Dalai Lama* (New York: Potala Corporation, 1983)
31. Girija Saklani, *Tibetan Refugees in India : A sociological Study of an Uprooted Community,* Book review, published in the *Tibet Journal,* 3, Winter 1978.
32. For details see, Melvyn Goldstein, *Ethnogenesis and Resource Competition among Tibetan refugees in South India: A New Face to the Indo-Tibetan Interface,* in James Fisher, (ed.) *Himalyan Anthropology,* (Mouton : The Hague, 1978
33. T. Samphel, no.9

5

IMPLICATIONS ON INDIA AS A HOST NATION

One should not be surprised to know that the survival of the Tibetan community is at stake not only in Chinese-controlled Tibet, but also in the host country, where they are in exile. With reference to India, where more than 80 per cent of the total Tibetan exilic community live in exile, the life of Tibetan refugees is not as smooth as it looks from outside. In reality most of these Tibetan settlements and scattered camps are suffering from internal problems, particularly the rapid growth of population among Tibetans, also problems in socio-economic adaptation which will now be discussed.

Firstly, apart from Chinese persecution, the destruction of Tibetan Buddhist monasteries in China compelled many young Tibetan Monks to come to India for religious education, to study Buddhism, Tibetan scriptures and cultural ethics, which is being denied in China. Secondly, in addition to the increasing number of births in exile, there is a constant flow of new Tibetans refugees from China since 1980, when travel restrictions from Tibet have become more relaxed.[1] Moreover, the free environment, freedom to practise democratic rights, education, medical facilities, attract Tibetans to escape to India. Thirdly, India provides the basic needs of Tibetans, mainly shelter and opportunity for an economic livelihood. The maximum number of Tibetan refugees living in India has been accommodated in various settlements with different rehabilitation sectors.

As a result of these factors, every month a few hundred new Tibetan refugees seek asylum in India.[2] In this way, the actual population might be double of the office population as many Tibetans who escape from Tibet do not register themselves with reception centre and prefer to live in scattered camps or independently. Obviously, this has led to a problem in socio-economic adaptation of the exiled Tibetan community within India. However, the elderly refugees do not face this problem since they have lived in India right from childhood and have worked and lived in the settlements. These people do not find any difficulty in surviving in India as refugees.

Whereas the younger generation at the present time as well as fresh arrivals from Tibet literally face a dilemma for survival.[3] With limited sources of income, they find it difficult to adjust and understand the critical situation of Tibetan refugees in the host country. The majority of them consist of either children or young people under the age of 25. Their presence has put a severe strain on the already fragile economy and the infra-structure of the settlements and facilities such as housing, sanitation, health clinic, and schools. This will compel them to scatter all over India, wherever it is possible and adapt themselves socially as well as economically in the respective areas. According to the report, over 11,000 of the total number of Tibetans who arrived in India and Nepal between 1959 and 1979 have never been provided with housing and the means of earning a living.[4]

For instance, they live in maximum numbers at Darjeeling, Kalimpong, Delhi-Majnu Ka Tila, even in Mumbai and in the southern part of India where the source of employment available to them is seasonal street trading, manual labour, and petty shop-keeping.

Due to the high literacy rate among Tibetans, the problem of unemployment among young Tibetans is persistently high and running at 20% in the 16 to 25 age bracket.[5] As a result, large numbers of educated youths are leaving the settlements in search of work outside. Moreover, it has been observed that in recent years, due to unemployment problem in settlements, Tibetans have preferred to live in scattered camps as employment prospects are better there than in the settlements. In the process, they do get accommodated wherever it is possible; in particular the business of selling sweaters attracts them, so that we can see maximum numbers of Tibetan refugees in this business. In this way, due to economic survival being at stake many young and able-bodied Tibetans have left the settlements and are living in unhygienic and crowded scattered camps at the cost of abandoning their children, the old people and the cultivation of land.

Due to this continuous migration from the settlements, the Tibetan administrators face another problem, that of running the risk of disintegration in the next generation. It is often said that rehabilitation of the second generation is more difficult than the first.

Moreover the urge for economic survival has led to children dropping out from the school and engaging themselves in petty work on the streets. These dropouts are generally immature children who are exposed to undesirable influences at an early age, creating for themselves a problem in social adaptation.

Along with this temporary economic prosperity and the funding and regular grants from foreign agencies the economic status of Tibetans automatically becomes higher in comparison to that the local villagers. This economic disparity between Tibetans and the local population sometimes leads to casual friction and conflict, sometimes over even small and irrelevant issues. Himachal Pradesh, especially is more sensitive in this matter, as the maximum numbers of Tibetans are living in both settlements and scattered camps in comparison with the rest of the states of India. For instance, in 1997-1998, there were continuous conflicts between the Tibetans and the local Indian communities particularly in the

Gaddi and Gujjar districts of Himachal Pradesh.[6] These conflicts were mainly due to the sharing of economic opportunities of livelihood in business, taxi-driving and shop-keeping. Most of the time, local Indians have come in mobs and ransacked Tibetan property; in retaliation, Tibetans have used violent methods and sometimes even killed responsible individuals. Sometimes, the rivalry among gangs of youths breaks out into violent physical clashes which, on many occasions have ended in murder, adding to law and order problems. In 1999 in Manali two murders took place due to a conflict between local people and Tibetans. The reason is still unknown.

It has also been observed that in Himachal Pradesh, where the Tibetan refugee settlements exist, the local population often harbours the feelings of social isolation within their own territory due to the presence of foreigners. Even the Dalai Lama accepted the fact and has reported in *The Times of India* (New Delhi) dated 4 July 1999 'Of course, there is some occasional fighting and even killings.' That is why even the Dalai Lama many times has announced that he would like to shift his Headquarters from Dharamsala to Karnataka or anywhere else in India.

In addition, issues like the struggle for an independent Tibet and campaigning against the Chinese authorities from Indian soil has led to an overall change in the Indian community's attitudes towards Tibetan refugees. Most of the time protest marches by Tibetans which generally begin in a peaceful manner, gradually turn into violence and shouting anti-Chinese slogans and criticizing Indian authorities openly. With these evidences, one can observe that not only persecution by the Chinese Government, but also the economic relations between the local Indians and Tibetans has compelled Tibetan refugees to live on the edge with no choice except to merely survive and exist.

At this point it is important look at the thesis of T.C. Palakshapa, titled *Tibetans in India: A Case Study of Mundgod*

Tibetans, (New Delhi: Sterling 1978). In this he mentioned for the first time that there was internal opposition from the Mysore State regarding handing over of land to Tibetan refugees. It had also created a hostile attitude against the Tibetans.

References

1. *Life in Exile* (Dharamsala : Tibetan Government in Exile, DIIR, 1997), p.5
2. This opinion based on Field Trips to Tibetan refugee camps during May–June 1999 in the Himachal Pradesh.
3. Ibid.
4. *Life in Exile*, p.14
5. Ibid., p. 11
6. No. 2

CONCLUSION

The South Asian countries have a historical tradition of generosity to absorb the aliens as well as refugees into their territory and live a life along with the feelings of fraternity and brotherhood. For instance, Pakistan accepted millions of refugees displaced as a result of partition of India in 1947 and hosted over three million Afghan refugees for almost twenty-five years since 1979. Bangladesh on the other hand had shown its willingness to receive its indigenous people the Chakmas from Chittagong Hill Tracts (CHT), from the state of Tripura, Arunachal Pradesh and Mizoram in India. On the other hand, it is finalizing plans to repatriate the remaining 24,000 of 250,000 Rohingya refugees to Myanmar, who sought refuge in Bangladesh twice in the last two decades. Over one lakh Bhutanese refugees are waiting in Nepal UNHCR camps at Beldangi in Damak district for repatriation to their homeland in Bhutan.

With reference to India, under the influence of Hindu philosophy of tolerance, secularism, non-violence, principles of Panch shool, implementation of middle path policy, peaceful solutions and so on India's experience with the refugees proves that it is a heaven for refugees of all over the world whether they are from Africa, Eastern Europe or Asia. India's long tradition of coping with refugee problems goes back to the partition of the subcontinent, when eight million refugees from the areas which are now Pakistan and Bangladesh, moved into India and were successfully integrated into the population. Even before this, during the World War II in

1941-42, many Indian origin refugees came from Myanmar (then Burma). Apart from receiving a large influx of Tibetan refugees, in 1971 during the Bangladesh crisis, it provided refuge to more than ten million refugees. Today India hosts over 50,000 Chakmas from Bangladesh and 70,000 Sri Lankan Tamil refugees and some 25,000 refugees of other nationalities mainly from Africa and few West Asian countries, including 25,000 Afghani refugees.

In reality, in modern days except India no other south Asian country welcomes refugees due to compound socio-economic and political problems. Whereas in India's case except the recent process of repatriation of Chakma refugees no other refugees seem to leave India willingly, not even Chakmas despite the recent Peace Agreement between the Governments of Bangladesh and India in 1997.

As far as Tibetan refugees are concerned, the exiled Tibetan community in India, has settled down whether in settlements or in scattered camps, and have equally adopted to the local areas and people. From Kashmir to deep in South Karnataka and Tamil Nadu, one can find Tibetans, selling woollen clothes and sweaters on the streets and involved in seasonal trading. However, the amalgamation process of Tibetans in various unscattered camps is much easier than the Tibetans in settlement camps as they can sell the goods on streets and involve themselves in any work such as labourers to a petty trader. This work requires communication in the local language which is picked up by Tibetans in order to survive economically as well as socially. Hence, we see that many Tibetans do speak even difficult languages like Tamil, Kannada and Marathi in the southern and western parts of India. Despite dry and hot weather and a plains topography, Tibetans have been able to achieve remarkable progress in work development in the same area where even the locals were unable to do it, for various reasons.

A good example of socio-economic adaptation of Tibetan refugees in India, is the Tibetan community settled in Sikkim and Darjeeling and Kalimpong hills. In these areas, apart from the cold and chilly weather and high mountains similar to Tibet, even the local population of Nepalese and Lepchas, accommodated them to such an extent, that Tibetans do not now consider themselves as refugees. Many marriages have taken place in this area. The affinity of Tibetans to this area is because it is just like their homeland, Tibet. It has become a home away from home. Therefore, one observes that although due to seasonal business and in search of economic livelihood, many Tibetans may move all over India, but they finally return to Darjeeling and Kalimpong, their homes during the off season.

The situation in overall Himachal Pradesh is however, quite disappointing, particularly at Dharamshala, Kullu, and Manali and to some extent in Arunachal Pradesh. The resentment of the local peasantry community like the Gujjar and Gaddi has developed some reservations about Tibetan refugees, who in the local language are recognized as *lamas*. The major grievance is regarding their economic prosperity, which has been achieved by Tibetans not only due to their hard work and business skill but also generous funding from Government of India and foreign agencies and individual donations. This makes the local Indians inferior in economic status, in comparison to Tibetan refugees. There are other factors which are equally responsible for developing this inferiority complex among local Indians, viz, in competitiveness in business, low literacy rate, lack of information, engagement in economic activity of tertiary sector and significantly, insensitivity in understanding the gravity of the problem of someone who is forcefully thrown out of his homeland. Thus, somehow, in the corner of their minds, local Indians fear that, Tibetans will not go back, but will settle down here permanently. One day they may even demand a separate homeland for themselves, outnumbering the locals. However this fear is baseless, and does not have any solid ground.

On the other hand Tibetans justify their survival as peaceful and do not develop any complex about the locals.

Their survival is harmless to the Indian community and society. One of the highest officials of the Tibetan Government in Exile argued that Tibetans are not citizens of this country; they are not fighting for any civil and political rights. To get employment, Tibetans do not apply for any government jobs. They do not even compete with Indians in the service sector. Moreover they do not snatch the economic opportunities from local Indians. On the contrary, an official argues that due to these Tibetan settlements, the Headquarters of Tibetan Government in Exile, and Palace of the Dalai Lama, in the barren and undeveloped area of Dharamsala has been converted into a most prosperous town, providing a big market for traders. The continuous flow of pilgrims, tourists and visitors also provides a lucrative business for travel and tourist agencies. This is true, to some extent, because the presence of Tibetan refugees in India, has developed and benefited the countryside, especially in Himachal Pradesh and Karnataka..

As compared to other refugees from the Indian sub-continent, the Tibetan refugees who are spread all over South Asia are living a peaceful life in South Asia. Their hard work, dedication and struggle in surviving and preserving of their own identity and culture, and the same time their respect for the local culture has made them quite successful and well-established over the last four decades. To some extent, adaptation of the local language has helped them to accommodate the sentiments of local people and adjust with the surrounding circumstances in order to survive. Except in Bhutan, as refugees, overall Tibetans in South Asia are very well adapted socially, economically and culturally.

Survival of the fittest, this Darwinian principle in its true sense is applicable to the Tibetan refugees who are spread all over India. The exilic Tibetan community, settled in settlements or in scattered camps, they are equally adapted in the local areas. From Kashmir to deep in South Karnataka and Tamil Nadu, one can find the Tibetans, who are selling woollen clothes and sweaters on streets and involved in seasonal trading. However, the amalgamation process of Tibetans in various scattered camps is much more easier than for the Tibetans in settlement camps. The obvious reason is since they are not settled in the settlements, in need of economic livelihood, Tibetans comes on the streets and involve themselves in any work as labourers to a petty trader, and sell seasonal items. This nature of work requires communication in local language that is picked up by Tibetans to survive economically as well as socially. Hence, we could see many Tibetans do speak difficult languages like Tamil, Kannada and Marathi in the southern and western part of India. Despite dry and hot weather and plain topography, Tibetans could achieve some how remarkable progress in work development in the same area in which the locals were unable to do it, because of many undesirable reasons.

To cite a good example of socio-economic adaptation of Tibetan refugees in India, the Tibetan community settled in Sikkim and Darjeeling and Kalimpong hills is the best of it. In these areas, apart from cold and chilly weather and high mountains which is similar to Tibet, even the local population Nepalese and Lepchas, accommodated them to such extent, Tibetans do not feel that they are refugees. Many marriages have taken place in this area. The affinity of Tibetans to this area is just like their homeland, Tibet. It has just become a home away from home.

However, the situation in overall Himachal Pradesh is quite disturbing particularly at Dharamshala, Kullu, Manali and to some extent in Arunachal Pradesh. The resentment of local peasantry community like Gujjar and Gaddi developed some reservations about Tibetan refugees, locally known as lamas. The major grievance is regarding their economic prosperity, which has been achieved by Tibetans not only due to their hard work and business skill but also generous funding from Government of India and foreign agencies and individual donations. This makes local Indians inferior in economic status, to most of the Tibetan refugees. There are other factors which are equally responsible for developing this inferiority complex among the local Indians, namely, in competitiveness in business, a low literacy rate, lack of information, engagement in economic activity of tertiary sector and finally, insensitivity to understand the gravity of the problem, when you are forcefully thrown out of your homeland. There is also as mentioned earlier, the Indians fear that, Tibetans will not go back and will settle here, permanently and one day will demand a separate homeland for themselves, outnumbering the locals.

Their survival is harmless to the Indian community and society one of the highest official of Tibetan Government in exile argued that Tibetans are not citizens of this country, they are not fighting for any civil and political rights. To get employment, Tibetans do not apply for any government jobs. They do not compete with Indians in the service sector. Tibetans do not snatch away the economic opportunities from local Indians.

But still the question of how many Tibetans would be willing to return to their mountain homeland with its uncertain prospects is now and will remain a matter for speculation.

At this point one can recall the prediction by Paul Grimes, in his reporting in the news paper *The New York Times,* dated June 16, 1961 from New Delhi:

> The Tibetans in India hope that some day they will be able to return to a homeland free of Communist interference. But they seem becoming increasingly aware that, until that day, it is necessary that they be absorbed profitably into the Indian economy.

Appendix-I

CONVENTION BETWEEN GREAT BRITAIN, CHINA AND TIBET, 1914

Has Majesty the King of the United Kingdom of Great Britain and Ireland and of the British Dominions beyond the Seas, Emperor of India, His Excellency the President of the Republic of China, and His Holiness the Dalai Lama of Tibet, being sincerely desirous to settle by mutual agreement, various questions concerning the interests of their several States on the continent of Asia, and further to regulate the relations of their several Governments, have resolved to conclude a Convention on this subject and have nominated for this purpose their respective Plenipotentiaries, that is to say :

His Majesty the King of the United Kingdom of Great Britain and Ireland and of the British Dominions beyond the Seas, Emperor of India :

Sir Arthur Henry McMahon, Knight Grand Cross of the Royal Victorian Order, Knight Commander of the Most Eminent Order of the Indian Empire, Companion of the Most Exalted Order of the Star of India, Secretary to the Government of India, Foreign and Political Department;

His Excellency the President of the Republic of China :

Monsieur Ivan Chen, Officer of the Order of the Chia, H.O.;

His Holiness the Dalai Lama of Tibet :

Lonchen Ga-den Shatra Pal-Jor Dorje;

Who having communicated to each other their respective full powers and finding them to be in good and due form have agreed upon the concluded the following Convention in eleven Articles :

Article 1

The Conventions specified in the Schedule to the present Convention shall, except in so far as they may have been modified by, or may be inconsistent with or repugnant to, any of the provisions of the present Convention, continue to be binding upon the High Contracting Parties.

Article 2

The Government of Great Britain and China recognising that Tibet is under the suzerainty of China, and recognising also the antonomy of Outer Tibet, engage to respect the territorial integrity of the country, and to abstain from interference in the administration of Outer Tibet (including the selection and installation, of the Dalai Lama), which shall remain in the hands of the Tibetan Government at Lhasa.

The Government of China engages not to convert Tibet into a Chinese province. The Government of Great Britain engages not to annex Tibet or any portion of it.

Article 3

Recognising the special interest of Great Britain, in virtue of the geographical position of Tibet, in the existence of an effective Tibetan Government, and in the maintenance of peace and order in the neighbourhood of the frontiers of India and adjoining States, the Government of China engages, except provided in Article 4 of this Convention, not to send troops into Outer Tibet, nor to station civil or military officers, not to establish Chinese colonies in the country. Should any such troops or officials remain in Outer Tibet at the date of the signature of this Convention, they shall be withdrawn within a period not exceeding three months.

The Government of Great Britain engages not to station military or civil officers in Tibet (except as provided in the Convention of September 7, 1904, between Great Britain and Tibet) nor troops (except the Agents' escorts), nor to establish colonies in that country.

Article 4

The foregoing Article shall not be held to preclude the continuance of the arrangement by which, in the past, a Chinese high official with suitable escort has been maintained at Lhasa, but it is hereby provided that the said escort shall in no circumstances exceed 300 men.

Article 5

The Government of China and Tibet engage that they will not enter into any negotiations or agreements regarding Tibet with one another, or with any other power, excepting such negotiations and agreements between Great Britain and Tibet as are provided for by the Convention of September 7, 1904, between Great Britain and Tibet and the Convention of April 27, 1906, between Great Britain and China.

Article 6

Article III of the Convention of April 27, 1906, between Great Britain and China is hereby cancelled, and it is understood that in Article IX(d) of the Convention of September 7, 1904, between Great Britain and Tibet the term "Foreign Power" does not include China.

Not less favourable treatment shall be accorded to British commerce than to the commerce of China or the most favoured nation.

Article 7

(a) The Tibet Trade Regulations of 1893 and 1908 are hereby cancelled.

(b) The Tibetan Government engages to negotiate with the British Government new Trade Regulations for Outer Tibet to give effect to Article II, IV and V of the Convention of September 7, 1904, between Great Britain and Tibet without delay; provided always that such Regulations shall in no way modify the present Convention except with the consent of the Chinese Government.

Article 8

The British Agent who resides at Gyantse may visit Lhasa with his escort whenever it is necessary to consult with the Tibetan Government regarding matters arising out of the Convention of September 7, 1904, between Great Britain and Tibet, which it has been found impossible to settle at Gyantse by correspondence or otherwise.

Article 9

For the purpose of the present Convention the borders of Tibet, and the boundary between Outer and Inner Tibet, shall be as shown in red and blue respectively on the map* attached hereto.

Nothing in the present Convention shall be held to prejudice the existing rights of the Tibetan Government in Inner Tibet, which include the power to select and appoint the high priests of monasteries and to retain full control in all matters affecting religious institutions.

Article 10

The English, Chinese and Tibetan texts of the present Convention have been carefully examined and found to correspond, but in the event of there being any difference

---

* Not published.

of meaning between them the English text shall be authoritative.

Article 11

The present Convention will take effect from the date of signature.

In Token whereof the respective Plenipotentiaries have signed and sealed this Convention, three copies in English, three in Chinese and three in Tibetans.

Done at Simla, this third day of July, A.D. one thousand nine hundred and fourteen, corresponding with the Chinese date, the third day of the seventh month of the third year of the Republic, and the Tibetan date, the tenth day of the fifth month of the Wood-Tiger Year.

Initial of the* LONCHEN SHATRA (*Initialled*) A.H.M.

Seal of the	Seal of the
Lonchen Shatra	British Plenipotentiary

Schedule

1. Convention between Great Britain and China relating to Sikkim and Tibet, signed at Calcutta the 17th March 1890.
2. Convention between Great Britain and Tibet, signed at Lhasa the 7th September 1904.
3. Convention between Great Britain and China respecting Tibet, signed at Peking the 27th April 1906.

The notes exchanges are to the following effect:

1. It is understood by the High Contracting Parties that Tibet forms part of Chinese territory.
2. After the selection and installation of the Dalai Lama by the Tibetan Government, the latter will notify the

* Owing to it not being possible to write initials in Tibetans, the mark of the Lonchen at this place is his signature.

installation to the Chinese Government, whose representative at Lhasa will then formally communicate to His Holiness the titles consistent with his dignity, which have been conferred by the Chinese Government.

3. It is also understood that the selection and appointment of all officers in Outer Tibet will rest with the Tibetan Government.
4. Outer Tibet shall not be represented in the Chinese Parliament or in any other similar body.
5. It is understood that the escorts attached to the British Trade Agencies in Tibet shall not exceed seventy five per centum of the escort of the Chinese Representative at Lhasa.
6. The Government of China is hereby released from its engagements under Article III of the Convention of March 17, 1890, between Great Britain and China to prevent acts of aggression from the Tibetan side of the Tibet-Sikkim frontier.
7. The Chinese high official referred to in Article 4 will be free to enter Tibet as soon as the terms of Article 3 have been fulfilled to the satisfaction of representatives of the three signatories to the Convention, who will investigate and report without delay.
8.

Initial of the LONCHEN SHATRA (*Initialled*) A.H.M.

Seal of the Lonchen Shatra	Seal of the British Plenipotentiary

Note

Whereas the Simla Convention itself after being initialled by the Chinese Plenipotentiary was not signed or ratified by the Chinese Government, it was accepted as binding by the two other parties as between themselves.

Appendix-II

THE AGREEMENT OF THE CENTRAL PEOPLE'S GOVERNMENT AND THE LOCAL GOVERNMENT OF TIBET ON MEASURES FOR THE PEACEFUL LIBERATION OF TIBET, 1951

Official Text of the Agreement signed in Peking on 23 May 1951, in the former Imperial Palace.

Preamble

The Tibetan nationality is one of the nationalities with a long history within the boundaries of China and, like many other nationalities, it has performed its glorious duty in the course of the creation and development of our great Motherland. But over the last one hundred years or more, imperialist forces penetrated into China, and in consequence also penetrated into the Tibetan region and carried out all kinds of deceptions and provocations. Like previous reactionary governments, the Kuomintang reactionary government continued to carry out a policy of oppressing and sowing dissension among the nationalities, causing division and disunity among the Tibetan people. And the local government of Tibet did not oppose the imperialist deceptions and provocations, and adopted an unpatriotic attitude toward our great Motherland. Under such conditions, the Tibetan nationality and people were plunged into the depths of enslavement and suffering.

In 1949, basic victory was achieved on a nationwide scale in the Chinese People's War of Liberation, the common domestic enemy of all nationalities – the Kuomintang reactionary government – was overthrown, and the common foreign enemy of all the nationalities – the aggressive imperialist forces – was driven out. On this basis, the founding of the People's Republic of China and of the Central People's Government was announced. In accordance with the Common Programme passed by the Chinese People's Political Consultative Conference, the Central People's Government declared that all nationalities within the boundaries of the People's Republic of China are equal, and that they shall establish unity and mutual aid and oppose imperialism and their own public enemies, so that the People's Republic of China will become a big fraternal and cooperative family, composed of all its nationalities, that within the big family of all nationalities of the People's Republic of China, national regional autonomy shall be exercised in areas where national minorities are concentrated, and all national minorities shall have freedom to develop their spoken and written languages and to preserve or reform their customs, habits, and religious beliefs, while the Central People's Government shall assist all national minorities to develop their political, economic, cultural and educational construction work. Since then, all nationalities within the country, with the exception of those in the areas of Tibet and Taiwan, have gained liberation. Under the unified leadership of the Central People's Government and the direct leadership of higher levels of People's Government, all national minorities are fully enjoying the right of national equality and have established, or are establishing, national regional autonomy.

In order that the influences of aggressive imperialist forces in Tibet might be successfully eliminated, the unification of the territory and sovereignty of the People's Republic of China accomplished, and national defence safeguarded; in order that the Tibetan nationality and people might be freed and return to the big family of the People's Republic of China to enjoy the same rights of national equality as all the other nationalities in the country and develop their political, economic, cultural, and educational work, the Central People's Government, when it ordered the People's Liberation Army to march into Tibet, notified the local government of Tibet to send delegates to the central authorities to conduct talks for the conclusion of an agreement on measures for the peaceful liberation of Tibet.

In the latter part of April 1951, the delegates with full powers of the local government of Tibet arrived in Peking. The Central People's Government appointed representatives with full powers to conduct talks on a friendly basis with the delegates with full powers of the local government of Tibet. As a result of these talks, both parties agreed to conclude this agreement and guarantee that it will be carried into effect.

1. The Tibetan people shall unite and drive out imperialist aggressive forces from Tibet; the Tibetan people shall return to the big family of the Motherland – the People's Republic of China.

2. The local government of Tibet shall actively assist the People's Liberation Army to enter Tibet and consolidate the national defence.

3. In accordance with the policy toward nationalities laid down in the Common Programme of the Chinese People's Political Consultative Conference, the Tibetan people have the right of exercising national regional autonomy under the unified leadership of the Central People's Government.

4. The central authorities will not alter the existing political system in Tibet. The central authorities also will not alter the established status, functions, and powers of the Dalai Lama. Officials of various ranks shall hold office as usual.

5. The established status, functions, and powers of the Panchen Ngoerhtehni shall be maintained.

6 By the established status, functions, and powers of the Dalai Lama and of the Panchen Ngoerhtehni are meant the status,

functions and powers of the Thirteenth Dalai Lama and of the Ninth Panchen Ngoerhtehni when they were in friendly and amicable relations with each other.

7. The policy of freedom of religious belief laid down in the Common Programme of the Chinese People's Political Consultative Conference shall be carried out. The religious beliefs, customs, and habits of the Tibetan people shall be respected, and lama monasteries shall be protected. The central authorities will not effect a change in the income of the monasteries.

8. Tibetan troops shall be reorganised by stages into the People's Liberation Army, and become a part of the national defence forces of the People's Republic of China.

9. The spoken and written language and school education of the Tibetan nationality shall be developed step by step in accordance with the actual conditions in Tibet.

10. Tibetan agriculture, livestock raising, industry, and commerce shall be developed step by step, and the people's livelihood shall be improved step by step in accordance with the actual conditions in Tibet.

11. In matters related to various reforms in Tibet, there will be no compulsion on the part of the central authorities. The local government of Tibet should carry out reforms of its own accord, and when the people raise demands for reform, they shall be settled by means of consultation with the leading personnel of Tibet.

12. In so far as former pro-imperialist and pro-Kuomintang officials resolutely sever relations with imperialism and the Kuomintang and do not engage in sabotage or resistance, they may continue to hold office irrespective of their past.

13. The people's Liberation Army entering Tibet shall abide by all the above-mentioned policies and shall also be fair in all buying and selling and shall not arbitrarily take a single needle or thread from the people.

14. The Central People's Government shall conduct the centralised handling of all external affairs of the area of Tibet; and there will be peaceful coexistence with neighbouring countries and establishment and development of fair commercial and trading

relations with them on the basis of equality, mutual benefit, and mutual respect for territory and sovereignty.

15. In order to ensure the implementation of this agreement, the Central People's Government shall set up a military and administrative committee and a military area headquarters in Tibet, and apart from the personnel sent there by the Central People's Government, shall absorb as many local Tibetan personnel as possible to take part in the work.

    Local Tibetan personnel taking part in the military and administrative committee may include patriotic elements from the local government of Tibet, various districts, and leading monasteries; the name list shall be drawn up after consultation between the representatives designated by the Central People's Government and the various quarters concerned, and shall be submitted to the Central People's Government for appointment.

16. Funds needed by the military and administrative committee, the military area headquarters, and the People's Liberation Army entering Tibet shall be provided by the Central People's Government. The local government of Tibet will assist the People's Liberation Army in the purchase and transport of food, fodder, and other daily necessities.

17. This agreement shall come into force immediately after signatures and seals are affixed to it.

Signed and sealed by :

Delegates with full powers of the Central People's Government:
Chief delegate: LI WEI-HAN

Tibetan chief delegate:

KALOON NGABOU NGAWANG JIGME

Peking May 23, 1951

Appendix-III

Sino-Indian Agreement on Tibet Signed on 29 April 1954

Preamble

Agreement between the Republic of India and the People's Republic of China on Trade and Intercourse between the Tibet Region of China and India.

The Government of the Republic of India and the Central People's Government of the People's Republic of China, being desirous of promoting trade and cultural intercourse between the Tibet Region of China and India and of facilitating pilgrimage and travel by the peoples of China and India, have resolved to enter into the present agreement based on the following principles:

(1) Mutual respect for each other's territorial integrity and sovereignty;

(2) Mutual non-aggression;

(3) Mutual non-interference in each other's internal affairs;

(4) Equality and mutual benefit; and

(5) Peaceful co-existence.

Article 1

The high contracting parties mutually agree to establish trade agencies :

1. The Government of India agrees that the Government of China may establish trade agencies at New Delhi, Calcutta and Kalimpong.

2. The Government of China agrees that the Government of India may establish trade agencies at Yatung, Gyantse and Gartok.

   The trade agencies of both parties shall be accorded the same status and same treatment. The trade agents of both parties shall enjoy freedom from arrest while exercising their functions and shall enjoy in respect of themselves, their wives and children who are dependent on them for livelihood, freedom from search.

   The trade agencies of both parties shall enjoy the privileges and immunities for couriers, mail bags and communications in code.

Article 2

The high contracting parties agree that traders of both countries known to be customarily and specifically engaged in trade between the Tibet Region and China and India may trade at the following places :

1. The Government of China agree to specify (1) Yatung, (2) Gyantse, and (3) Phari as markets for trade. The Government of India agree that trade may be carried on in India, including places like (1) Kalimpong, (2) Siliguri, and (3) Calcutta, according to customary practice.

2. The Government of China agree to specify (1) Gartok, (2) Pulanchung (Taklakot), (3) Gyanimakhargo, (4) Gyantmachakra, (5) Ramura, (6) Dongbra, (7) Pulingsumdo, (8) Nabra, (9) Shangtse and (10) Tashigong as markets for trade.

   The Government of India agree that in future, when in accordance with the development and need of trade between the Ari district of the Tibet Region of China and India, it has become necessary to specify markets for trade in the corresponding district in India adjacent to the Ari district of the Tibet Region of China, they will be prepared to consider on the basis of equality and reciprocity to do so.

Article 3

The high contracting parties agree that pilgrimages by religious believers of the two countries shall be carried on in accordance with the following provisions :

1. Pilgrims from India of Lamaist, Hindu and Buddhist faiths may visit Kang Rimpoche (Kailas) and Mavan Tso (Manasarovar) in the Tibet Region of China in accordance with custom.
2. Pilgrims from the Tibet Region of China of Lamaist and Buddhist faiths may visit Banaras, Sarnath, Gaya, and Sanchi in India in accordance with custom.
3. Pilgrims customarily visiting Lhasa may continue to do so in accordance with custom.

Article 4

Traders and pilgrims of both countries may travel by the following passes and route :

(1) Shipki La, (2) Mana pass, (3) Niti pass, (4) Kungri Bingri pass, (5) Dharma pass and (6) Lipu Laku pass. Also, the customary route leading to Tashigong along the valley of the Shangatsungpu (Indus) River may continue to be traversed in accordance with custom.

Article 5

For travelling across the border, the high contracting parties agree that diplomatic personnel, officials and nationals of the two countries shall hold passports issued by their own respective countries and visaed by the other party except as provided in paragraphs 1, 2, 3, and 4 of this Article.

1. Traders if both countries known to be customarily and specifically engaged in trade between the Tibet Region of China and India, their wives and children, who are dependent on them for livelihood and their attendants will be allowed entry for purposes of trade into India or the Tibet Region of China,

as the case may be, in accordance with custom on the production of certificates duly issued by the local government of their own country or by its duly authorised agents and examined by the border checkposts of the other party.

2. Inhabitants of the border districts of the two countries, who cross borders to carry on petty trade or to visit friends and relatives, may proceed to the border districts of the other party as they have customarily done heretofore and need not be restricted to the passes and route specified in Article 4 above and shall not be required to hold passports, visas or permits.

3. Porters and mule-team drivers of the two countries who cross the border to perform necessary transportation services need not hold passports issued by their own country, but shall only hold certificates good for a definite period of time (three months, half a year or one year) duly issued by the local government of their own country or by its duly authorised agents and produce them for registration at the border checkposts of the other party.

4. Pilgrims of both countries need not carry documents of certification but shall register at the border checkposts of the other party and receive a permit for pilgrimage.

5. Notwithstanding the provisions of the foregoing paragraphs of this Article, either Government may refuse entry to any particular person.

6. Persons who enter the territory of the other party in accordance with the foregoing paragraphs of this Article may stay within its territory only after complying with the procedures specified by the other party.

Article 6

The present Agreement shall come into effect upon ratification by both Governments and shall remain in force for eight years. Extension of the present Agreement may be negotiated by the two parties if either party requests for its six months prior to the expiry of the Agreement and the request is agreed to by the other party.

Done in duplicate in Peking on the 29th of April, 1954, in the Chinese, Hindi and English languages, all texts being equally valid.

Plenipotentiary of the Central People's Government of the People's Republic of China –
CHANG HAN-FU

Plenipotentiary of the Government of the Republic of India –
NEDYAM RAGHAVAN

Appendix-IV

DALAI LAMA SPEAKS ON HIS OWN BEHALF

At his first press conference in India, on 20 June 1959 at Mussoorie, the Dalai Lama told the story of the Tibetan rebellion in his own words. The following statement was issued to the newspapermen before the Dalai answered questions :

Ever since my arrival in India, I have been receiving almost every day sad and distressing news of the suffering and inhuman treatment of my people. I have heard almost daily, with a heavy heart, of their increasing agony and affliction, their harassment and persecution and of the terrible deportation and execution of innocent men. These have made me realise forcibly that the time has manifestly arrived when in the interests of my people and religion and to save them from the danger of near-annihilation, I must not keep silent any longer but must frankly and plainly tell the world the truth about Tibet and appeal to the conscience of all peace-loving and civilised nations.

The Tragic Happenings

To understand and appreciate the significance and implication of the recent tragic happenings in Tibet, it is necessary to refer to the main events which has occurred in the country since 1950. It is recognised by every independent observer that Tibet had virtually been independent by enjoying and exercising all rights of sovereignty, whether internal or external. This has also been impliedly admitted by the Communist Government of China, for the very structure, terms and conditions of the so-called agreement of 1951 conclusively show that it was an agreement between two independent and sovereign States. It follows, therefore, that when the Chinese armies violated the territorial integrity of Tibet they were committing a flagrant act of aggression. The agreement which followed the invasion of Tibet was also thrust upon its people and government by the threat of arms. It was never accepted by them of their own free will. The consent of the government was secured under duress and at the point of the bayonet. My representatives were compelled to sign the agreement under threat of further military operations against Tibet by the invading armies of China leading to utter ravage and ruin of the country. Even the Tibetan seal which was affixed to the agreement was not the seal of my representatives but a seal copied and fabricated by the Chinese authorities in Peking, and kept in their possession ever since.

Reign of Terror

While I and my government did not voluntarily accept the agreement, we were obliged to acquiesce in it and decided to abide by the terms and conditions in order to save my people and country from the danger of total destruction. It was, however, clear from the very beginning that the Chinese had no intention of carrying out the agreement. Although they had solemnly undertaken to maintain my status and power as the Dalai Lama, they did not lose any opportunity to undermine my authority and sow dissensions among my people. In fact, they compelled me, situated as I was, to dismiss my Prime Ministers under threat of their execution without trial because they had in all honesty and sincerity resisted the unjustified usurpation of power by the representatives of the Chinese Government in Tibet. Far from carrying out the agreement, they began deliberately to pursue a course of policy which was diametrically opposed to the terms and conditions which they had themselves laid down.

Thus commenced a reign a terror which finds few parallels in the history of Tibet. Forced labour and compulsory exactions, a systematic persecution of the people, plunder and confiscation of property belonging to individuals and monasteries, and execution of certain leading men in Tibet – these are the glorious achievements of the Chinese rule in Tibet. During all this time, patiently and sincerely I endeavoured to appease my people and to calm down their feelings and at the same time tried my best to persuade the Chinese authorities in Lhasa to adopt a policy of conciliation and friendliness. In spite of repeated failures, I persisted in this policy till the last day when it became impossible for me to render any useful service to my people by remaining in Tibet. It is in these circumstances that I was obliged to leave my country in order to save it from further danger and disaster.

Neutral Investigation

I wish to make it clear that I have made these assertions against the Chinese officials in Tibet in the full knowledge of their gravity because I know them to be true. Perhaps the Peking Government are not fully aware of the facts of the situation, but if they are not prepared to accept these statements, let them agree to an investigation on the point by an international commission. On our part, I and my government will readily agree to abide by the verdict of such an impartial body.

Chinese Break Promises

It is necessary for me to add that before I visited India in 1956, it had become increasingly clear to me that my policy of amity and tolerance had totally failed to create any impression on the representatives of the Chinese Government in Tibet. Indeed, they had frustrated every measure adopted by me to remove the bitter resentment felt by my people and to bring about a peaceful atmosphere in the country for the purpose of carrying out the necessary reforms. As I was unable to do anything for the benefit of my people, I had practically made up my mind when I came to India not to return to Tibet until there was manifest change in the attitude of the Chinese authorities. I, therefore, sought the advice of the Prime Minister of India, who has always shown me unfailing kindness and consideration. After his talk with the Chinese Prime Minister and on the strength of the assurances given by him on behalf of China, Mr. Nehru advised me to change my decision. I followed his advice and returned to Tibet in the hope that conditions would change substantially for the better, and I have no doubt that my hopes would have been realised if the Chinese authorities had on their part carried out the assurances which the Chinese Prime Minister had given to the Prime Minister of India. It was, however, painfully clear soon after my return that the representatives of the Chinese Government had no intention to adhere to their promises. The natural and inevitable result was that the situation steadily grew worse until it became impossible to control the spontaneous upsurge of my people against the tyranny and oppression of the Chinese authorities.

Not Opposed to Reforms

At this point I wish to emphasize that I and my government have never been opposed to the reforms which are necessary in the social, economic and political systems prevailing in Tibet. We have no desire to disguise that fact that ours is an ancient society and that we must introduce immediate changes in the interests of the people of Tibet. In fact, during the last nine years several reforms were proposed by me and my government, but every time these measures were strenuously opposed by the Chinese in spite of popular demand for them, with the result that nothing was done for the betterment of the social and economic conditions of the people. In particular, it was my earnest desire that the system of land tenure should be radically changed without further delay and the large landed estates acquired by the State on payment of compensation for distribution amongst the tillers of the soil. But the Chinese authorities deliberately put every obstacle in the way of carrying out this just and reasonable reform. I desire to lay stress on the fact that we, as firm believers in Buddhism, welcome change and progress consistent with the genius of our people and the rich traditions of our country, but the people of Tibet will stoutly resist any victimisation, sacrilege and plunder in the name of reforms, a policy which is now being enforced by the representatives of the Chinese Government in Lhasa.

A Clear Picture

I have attempted to present a clear and unvarnished picture of the situation in Tibet. I have endeavoured to tell the entire civilised world the real truth about Tibet, the truth which must ultimately prevail, however strong the forces of evil may appear to be today. I also wish to declare that we Buddhists firmly and steadfastly believe in peace and desire to live in peace with all the peoples and countries of the world. Although recent actions and policies of the Chinese authorities in Tibet have created strong feelings of bitterness and resentment against the Government of China, we, Tibetans, lay and monk alike, do not cherish any feelings of enmity and hatred against the great Chinese people. We wish to live in peace and ask for peace and goodwill from all the countries of the world. I and my government are, therefore, fully prepared to welcome a peaceful and amicable solution of the present tragic problem, provided that such a solution guarantees the preservation of the rights and powers which Tibet has enjoyed and exercised without any interference prior to 1950. We must also insist on the creation of a favourable climate by the immediate adoption of the essential measures as a condition precedent to negotiations for a peaceful settlement. We ask for peace and for a peaceful settlement, but we must also ask for the maintenance of the status and the rights of our State and people. To you, gentlemen of the press, I and my people owe a great debt of gratitude for all that you have done to assist us in our struggle for survival and freedom. Your sympathy and support have given us courage and strengthened our determination. I confidently hope that you will continue to lend the weight of your influence to the cause of peace and freedom which the people of Tibet are fighting today. Gentlemen, I thank you, one and all; on behalf of my people as well as on my own behalf.

Appendix-V

Dalai Lama Takes Tibet Back to the UN

The text of the cable sent by the Dalai Lama to the United Nations Secretary-General urging UN intervention in Tibet on humanitarian grounds. The cable reached UN headquarters on 9 September 1959, and was circulated by the Secretary-General to member nations.

Your Excellency Mr. Hammarskjoeld:

Kindly refer to the proceedings of the General Committee of the United Nations General Assembly held on Friday, 24th November, 1950, at which it was resolved that the consideration of El Salvador's complaint against the invasion of Tibet by foreign forces should be adjourned in order to give the parties the opportunity to arrive at a peaceful settlement. It is with the deepest regret that I am informing you that the act of aggression by Chinese forces has not terminated. On the contrary, the area of aggression has been substantially extended with the result that practically the whole of Tibet is under the occupation of the Chinese forces. I and my Government have made several appeals for a peaceful and friendly settlement, but so far these appeals have been completely ignored. In these circumstances and in view of the inhuman treatment and crimes against humanity and religion to which the people of Tibet are being subjected, I solicit immediate intervention of the United Nations and consideration by the General Assembly on its own initiative of the Tibetan issue, which has been adjourned. In this connection, I and my Government wish to emphasize that Tibet was a sovereign State at the time when her territorial integrity was violated by the Chinese armies in 1950. In support of this contention, the Government of Tibet urges the following:

1. No power or authority was exercised by the Government of China in or over Tibet since the declaration of independence by the 13th Dalai Lama in 1912.

2. The sovereign status of Tibet during this period finds conclusive evidence in the fact that the Government of Tibet concluded as many as five international agreements immediately before and during these years.

3. The Government of Tibet take their stand on the Anglo-Tibetan Convention of 1914 which recognised the sovereign status of Tibet and accorded the same position to the Tibetan plenipotentiary as was given to the representatives of Great Britain and China. It is true this convention imposed certain restrictions on the external sovereignty of Tibet, but these did not deprive her of her international position. Moreover, these restrictions ceased to have any effect on the transfer of power to India.

4. There is no valid and subsisting international agreement under which Tibet or any other Power recognises Chinese suzerainty.

5. The sovereign status of Tibet is equally evident from the fact that during the Second World War Tibet insisted on maintaining her neutrality and only allowed the transport of non-military goods from India to China through Tibet. This position was accepted by the Government of Great Britain and China.

6. The sovereign status of Tibet has also been acknowledged by other Powers. In 1948, when a trade delegation from the Government of Tibet visited India, France, Italy, the United Kingdom and the United States of America, the passports issued by the Tibetan Government were accepted by the Governments of these countries.

Your Excellency, My Government also solicit immediate intervention of the United Nations on humanitarian grounds.

Since their violation of the territorial integrity of Tibet, the Chinese forces have committed the following offences against the universally accepted laws of international conduct:

(1) They have dispossessed thousands of Tibetans of their properties and deprived them of every source of livelihood and thus driven them to death and desperation;

(2) Men, women and children have been forced into labour gangs and made to work on military construction without payment or on nominal payment;

(3) They have adopted cruel and inhuman measures for the purpose of sterilizing Tibetan men and women with a view to the total extermination of the Tibetan race ;

(4) Thousands of innocent people of Tibet have been brutally massacred;

(5) There have been many cases of murder of leading citizens of Tibet without any cause or justification;

(6) Every attempt has been made to destroy our religion and culture. Thousands of monasteries have been razed to the ground and sacred images and articles of religion completely destroyed. Life and property are no longer safe and Lhasa, the capital of the State, is now a dead city.

The sufferings, which my people are undergoing, are beyond description and it is imperatively necessary that this wanton and ruthless murder of my people should be immediately brought to an end.

It is in these circumstances that I appeal to you [Mr. Hammarskjoeld] and the United Nations in the confident hope that our appeal will receive the consideration which it deserves.

Appendix-VI

UN Assembly Passes Tibet Resolution

On October 21, 1959, the United Nations adopted a joint Malay-Irish resolution on Tibet, which without naming the Chinese People's Republic, deplored the violation of the fundamental human rights in Tibet and called for their restoration.

Forty-five nations supported the resolution. Nine opposed it. Twenty-six countries, including India, abstained. Two, Guinea and Costa Rica, were absent.

The following is the text of the resolution: The General Assembly,

Recalling the principles regarding fundamental human rights and freedom set out in the Charter of the United Nations and in the Universal Declaration of Human Rights adopted by the General Assembly on December 10, 1948,

Considering that the fundamental human rights and freedoms to which the Tibetan people, like all others, are entitled include the right to civil and religious liberty for all without distinction,

Mindful also of the distinctive cultural and religious heritage of the people of Tibet and of the autonomy which they have traditionally enjoyed,

Gravely concerned at reports, including the official statements of His Holiness the Dalai Lama, to the effect that the fundamental human rights and freedoms of the people of Tibet have been forcibly denied them,

Deploring the effect of these events in increasing international tensions and embittering the relations between peoples at a time when earnest and positive efforts are being made by responsible leaders to reduce tension and improve international relations,

1. Affirms its belief that respect for the principles of the Charter and of the Universal Declaration of Human Rights is essential for the evolution of a peaceful world order based on the rule of law,
2. Calls for respect for the fundamental human rights of the Tibetan people and for their distinctive cultural and religious life.

The following is the voting analysis:

Yes (45) : Argentina, Australia, Austria, Bolivia, Brazil, Canada, Chile, Kuomintang China, Colombia, Cuba, Denmark, Ecuador, El Salvador, Malaya, Greece, Guatemala, Haiti, Honduras, Ice-land, Iran, Ireland, Israel, Italy, Japan, Jordan, Laos, Liberia, Luxembourg, Mexico, Netherlands, New Zealand, Nicaragua, Norway, Pakistan, Panama, Paraguay, Peru, the Philippines, Sweden, Thailand, Tunisia, Turkey, the U.S., Uruguay, Venezuela

No. (9): Albania, Bulgaria, White Russia, Czechoslovakia, Hungary, Poland, Rumania, Ukraine, Soviet Union

Abstentions (26) : Afghanistan, Belgium, Britain, Burma, Cambodia, Ceylon, Dominican Republic, Ethiopia, Finland, France, Ghana, India, Indonesia, Iraq, the Lebanon, Lybia, Morocco, Nepal, Portugal, Saudi Arabia, Spain, Sudan, South Africa, the United Arab Republic, Yemen, Yugoslavia. *Absent* (2) : Guinea, Costa Rica.

Appendix-VII

CITIZENSHIP IN THE CONSTITUTION OF INDIA

Part II – CITIZENSHIP

5. Citizenship at the commencement of the Constitution
6. Rights of citizenship of certain persons who have migrated to India from Pakistan
7. Rights of citizenship of certain migrants to Pakistan
8. Rights of citizenship of certain persons of Indian origin residing outside India.
9. Persons voluntarily acquiring citizenship of a foreign State not to be citizen.
10. Continuance of the rights of citizenship.
11. Parliament to regulate the right of citizenship by law

Part II– CITIZENSHIP

5. At the commencement of this Constitution, every person who has his domicile in the territory of India and –

    (a) who was born in the territory of India; or

    (b) either of whose parents was born in the territory of India; or

    (c) who has been ordinarily resident in the territory of India for not less than five years immediately preceding such commencement, shall be a citizen of India.

6. Notwithstanding anything in article 5, a person who has migrated to the territory of India from the territory now included in Pakistan shall be deemed to be a citizen of India at the commencement of this Constitution if -

   (a) he or either of his parents or any of his grand-parents was born in India as defined in the Government of India Act, 1935 (as originally enacted); and \

   (b) (i) in the case where such person has so migrated before the nineteenth day of July, 1948, he has been ordinarily resident in the territory of India since the date of his migration, or

   (ii) in the case where such person has so migrated on or after the nineteenth day of July, 1948, he has been registered as a citizen of India by an officer appointed in that behalf by the Government of the Dominion of India on an application made by him there for to such officer before the commencement of this Constitution in the form and manner prescribed by the Government:

   Provided that no person shall be so registered unless he has been resident in the territory of India for at least six months immediately preceding the date of his application.

7. Notwithstanding anything in articles 5 and 6, a person who has after the first day of March, 1947, migrated from the territory of India to the territory now included in Pakistan shall not be deemed to be a citizen of India :

   Provided that nothing in this article shall apply to a person who, after having so migrated to the territory now included in Pakistan, has returned to the territory of India under a permit for resettlement or permanent return issued by or under the authority of any law and every such person shall for the purposes of clause (b) of article 6 be deemed to have migrated to the territory of India after the nineteenth day of July, 1948.

8. Notwithstanding anything in article 5, any person who or either of whose parents or any of whose grand-parents was born in India as defined in the Government of India Act, 1935 (as originally enacted), and who is ordinarily residing in any country outside India as so defined shall be deemed to be a citizen of India if he has been registered as a citizen of India by the diplomatic or consular representative of India in the country where he is for the time being residing on an application made

by him therefor to such diplomatic or consular representative, whether before or after the commencement of this Constitution, in the form and manner prescribed by the Government of the Dominion of India or the Government of India.

9. No person shall be a citizen of India by virtue of article 5, or be deemed to be a citizen of India by virtue of article 6 or article 8, if he has voluntarily acquired the citizenship of any foreign State.

10. Every person who is or is deemed to be a citizen of India under any of the foregoing provisions of this Part shall, subject to the provisions of any law that may be made by Parliament, continue to be such citizen.

11. Nothing in the foregoing provisions of this Part shall derogate from the power of Parliament to make any provision with respect to the acquisition and termination of citizenship and all other matters relating to citizenship.

Appendix-VIII

THE CITIZENSHIP ACT, 1955

NO. 57 OF 1955

[30th December, 1955]

An act to provide for the acquisition and determination of Indian citizenship.

BE it enacted by Parliament in the Sixth Year of the Republic of India as follows –

1. This Act may be called the Citizenship Act, 1955.

2. (1) In this Act, unless the context otherwise requires –

   (a) "a Government of India" means the Central Government or a State Government;

   (b) "citizen", in relation to a country specified in the First Schedule, means a person who, under the citizenship or nationality law for the time being in force in that country, is a citizen or national of that country;

   (c) "citizenship or nationality law", in relation to a country specified in the First Schedule, means an enactment of the legislature of that country which, at the request of the Government of that country, the Central Government may, by notification in the Official Gazette, have declared to be an enactment making provision for the citizenship or nationality of that country:

Provided that no such notification shall be issued in relation to the Union of South Africa except with the previous approval of both Houses of Parliament;

(d) "Indian consulate" means the office of any consular officer of the Government of India where a register of births is kept, or where there is no such office, such office as may be prescribed;

(e) "minor" means a person who has not attained the age of eighteen years;

(f) "person" does not include any company or association or body of individuals, whether incorporated or not;

(g) "prescribed" means prescribed by rules made under this Act;

(h) "undivided India" means India as defined in the Government of India Act, 1935, as originally enacted.

(2) For the purpose of this Act, a person born aboard a registered ship or aircraft, or aboard an unregistered ship or aircraft of the Government of any country, shall be deemed to have been born in the place in which the ship or aircraft was registered or, as the case may be, in that country.

(3) Any reference in this Act to the status or description of the father of a person at the time of that person's birth shall, in relation to a person born after the death of his father, be construed as a reference to the status or description of the father at the time of the father's death; and where that death occurred before, ad the birth occurs after, the commencement of this Act, the status or description which would have been applicable to the father had he died after the commencement of this Act shall be deemed to be the status or description applicable to him at the time of his death.

(4) For the purposes of this Act, a person shall be deemed to be of full age if he is not a minor, and of full capacity if he is not of unsound mind.

Acquisition of Citizenship

3. (1) Except as provided in sub-section (2) of this section, every person born in India on or after the 26th January, 1950, shall be a citizen of India by birth.

(2) A person shall not be such a citizen by virtue of this section if at the time of his birth –

(a) his father possesses such immunity from suits and legal process as is accorded to an envoy of a foreign sovereign power accredited to the President of India and is not a citizen of India; or

(b) his father is an enemy alien and the birth occurs in a place then under occupation by the enemy

4. (1) A person born outside India on or after the 26th January, 1950, shall be citizen of India by descent if his father is a citizen of India at the time of his birth :

Provided that if the father of such a person was a citizen of India by descent only, that person shall not be a citizen of India by virtue of this section unless

(a) his birth is registered at an Indian consulate within one year of its occurrence or the commencement of this Act, whichever is later, or, with the permission of the Central Government, after the expiry of the said period; or

(b) his father is, at the time of his birth, in service under a Government in India.

(2) If the Central Government so directs, a birth shall be deemed for the purpose of this section to have been registered with its permission, notwithstanding that its permission was not obtained before the registration.

(3) For the purpose of the proviso to sub-section (1), any male person born outside undivided India who was, or was deemed to be a citizen of India at the commencement of the Constitution shall be deemed to be a citizen of India by descent only.

5. (1) Subject to the provisions of this section and such conditions and restrictions as may be prescribed, the prescribed authority may, on application made in this behalf, register as a citizen of India any person who is not already such citizen by virtue of the Constitution or by virtue of any of the other provisions of this Act and belongs to any of the following categories-

(a) persons of Indian origin who are ordinarily resident in India and have been so resident for six months immediately before making an application for registration;

(b) persons of Indian origin who are ordinarily resident in any country or place outside undivided India;

(c) women who are, or have been, married to citizens of India;

(d) minor children of persons who are citizens of Indian; and

(e) persons of full age and capacity who are citizens of a country specified in the First Schedule:

Provided that in prescribing the condition ad restrictions subject to which persons of any such country may be registered as citizens of India under this clause, the Central Government shall have due regard to the conditions subject to which citizens of that country by registration.

Explanation – For the purposes of this sub-section, a person shall be deemed to be of Indian origin if he, or either of his parents, or any of his grand-parents, was born in undivided India.

(2) No person being of full age shall be registered as a citizen of India under sub-section (1) until he has taken the oath of allegiance in the form specified in the Second Schedule.

(3) No person who has renounced, or has been deprived of, his Indian citizenship, or whose Indian citizenship has terminated, under this Act shall be registered as a citizen of India under sub-section (1) except by order of the Central Government.

(4) The Central Government may, if satisfied that there are special circumstances justifying such registration, cause any minor to be registered as a citizen of India.

(5) A person registered under this section shall be a citizen of India by registration as from the date on which he is so registered; and a person registered under the provisions of clause (b) (ii) of article 6 or article 8 of the Constitution shall be deemed to be a citizen of India by registration as from the commencement of the Constitution or the date on which he was so registered, whichever may be later.

6. (1) Where an application is made in the prescribed manner by any person of full age and capacity who is not a citizen of a country specified in the First Schedule for the grant of a certificate of naturalization to him, the Central Government may, if satisfied that the applicant is qualified for naturalization under the provisions of the Third Schedule, grant to him a certificate of naturalization:

Provided that, if in the opinion of the Central Government, the applicant is a person who has rendered distinguished service to the cause of science, philosophy, art, literature, world peace or human progress generally, it may waive all or any of the condition specified in the Third Schedule.

(2) The person to whom a certificate of naturalization is granted under sub-section (1) shall, on taking the oath of allegiance in the form specified in the Second Schedule, be a citizen of India by naturalization as from the date on which that certificate is granted.

7. If any territory becomes a part of India, the Central Government may, by order notified in the Official Gazette, specify the persons who shall be citizens of India by reason of their connection with that territory; and those persons shall be citizens of India as from the date to be specified in the order.

BIBLIOGRAPHY

Books

Addy Prernen, *Tibet on the Imperial Chessboard*, (New Delhi: Academic Publishers, 1984).

Arakeri, A.V., *Tibetans in India : The Uprooted People and their Cultural transplantation*, (Delhi : Reliance, 1980).

Arpi Claude, *The Fate of Tibet: When Big Insects Eat Small Insects* (New Delhi: Har Anand, 1999)

Banerjee, Brojendra Nath, *India's aid to its neighbouring countries*, (New Delhi : Select Books, 1982).

Barber, Noel, *The Flight of the Dalai Lama* (London : Hodder and Stoughton, 1960).

Barker Carol, *The Tibetans : Life in Exile* (London : Mantra in association with Tibet Foundation, 1998).

Bell Charles, *Tibet Past & Present* (London : OUP 1968).

Bhat, Sudhakar, *India and China* (New Delhi : Popular Book Service, 1967).

Breaking Silence, In Support of Tibet (India : Friends of Tibet and TYC, 2000).

Burman, Bina Roy, *Religion and Politics in Tibet* (New Delhi : Vikas Pub., 1979)

Cassinelli and Ekvall R.B., *A Tibetan Principality : The Political System of Sa skya* (Ithaca : Cornell University Pren, 1969).

Central Tibetan Administration of H.H. the Dalai Lama, Council for Home Affairs, (Dharamsala : n.a.)

Chimni, B.S. (Ed.); *International Refugee Law: A Reader*, (New Delhi: Sage 2001)

China's Bid for World Power :(New Delhi : Col, MEA, East Asia Research & Co-ordination Division, May 1963).

Choudhary Deba Prosad, *Trade and Politics in the Himalaya – Karakoram Borderlands* (Hyderabad : Orient Longman, 1996)

Corlin Class, *The Nation in Your Mind: Continuity and change among Tibetan Refugees in Nepal* (University of Gofeberg : Ph.D. Thesis, Pub., 1975).

Dalai Lama, *My Land and My People* (The autobiography of His Holiness the Dalai Lama) (London : Weildenfield & Nicolson, 1962).

Dalai Lama, *Tibet, China and The World, A Compilation of Interviews* (Dharamsala : Narthang Pub., 1989).

Dargyay Eva. K., *Tibetan Village Communities : Structure and change* (New Delhi : Vikas Publishing House, 1982).

Das Chandra S., *Journey to Lhasa and Central Tibet* (New Delhi : Manjushri Pub. House, 1970).

Datta C.C., *Ladakh and Western Himalayan, Himalayan Politics ; Bengal : Past and Present* (Vol. LXXXXIX of I, 1970 Calcutta)

Devoe, Dorsh Marie, *Survival of a Refugee Culture: The Longterm gift exchange between Tibetan refugees and donors in India* (Michigan: UMI Ph.D. Dissertation, 1986).

Dharamsala and Beijing, *Initiatives and Correspondence 1981 – 1993* (Dharamsala: DIIR, 1996).

Donnet Pierre Antonie, *Tibet : Survival in Question* (Delhi : OUP, 1994). Translated by Tica Broch (London : Zed Books Ltd.).

Education in Exile : Building Our Future Through Education : An Informative Guide (Dharamsala, H.P. 1998)

Enforcing Loyalty : (Dharamsala : TCHRD, 2001).

Fearless Voices: Accounts of Tibetan Former Political Prisoners (Dharamsala : TCHRD, February 1998).

Fisher M.W., Rose L.E. & Hunttenback R.A., *Himalayan Battleground* (New York, 1963).

Forbes, Ann Armbrecht, *Settlements of Hope: An account of Tibetan Refugees in Nepal* (Cambridge: Cultural Survival, 1989).

Franck, AH., *A History of Western Tibet* (London: 1907).

Frechette, Ann, *Statelessness and Power: Transformational entitlements among Tibetan exiles in Kathmandu, Nepal.* (Harvard University, Ph.D. Thesis,UMI, 1997).

From the Roof the World: Refugees of Tibet (Berkeley: Dharma Publishing, 1992).

Furer Haimendorf, Christoph Von, *The Renaissance of Tibetan Civilization* (Delhi : Oxford University Pub. 1990)

Ghosh, Suchita, *Tibet in Sino – Indian Relations 1899 – 1914* (New Delhi : Sterling Pub. Pvt. Ltd. 1977).

Gold Peter, *Tibetan Reflection: Life in Tibetan Refugee Community* (London : Wisdom, 1984).

Goldstein, Melvyn, William Sibenschuh and Tashi Tsering, *The Struggle for Modern Tibet : The Autobiography of Tashi Tsering* (New York : M.E. Sharpe, 1997).

Gordon, T.E., *The Roof of the World* (Edinburgh, 1876).

Grunfeld, Tom A, *The Making of Modern Tibet* (Bombay : Oxford University Press, 1987).

Hampton, Janie, (Ed.); *Internally Displaced People: A Global Survey,* (London: Earth scan Pub. Ltd. 1997)

Holdich, T., *Tibet the Mysterious* (London, 1908).

Hutheesing Raja. (Ed.), *Tibet Fights for Freedom* (Bombay : Orient Longmans, 1960)

Indian Leaders on Tibet (Dharamsala : DIIR, CTA, 1998).

Indian Press on India – Tibet – China Relations: Selections from Press (New Delhi : TPPCR, 1997),

Information office, Tibet Under Chinese Communist Rule : A Compilation of Refugee Statement 1950 – 1975. (Dharamsala : DIIR, 1976).

Jain Girilal, *Panchsheela and After* (Bombay: Asia Publishing House, and New York: Taplinger Pub. Co. 1960) (pp. 230)

Krull, Germaine, *Tibetans in India* (Delhi : Allied, 1968)

Lang-Sims. Lois. *The Presence of Tibet,* (London: Creset Press, 1963).

Lattimore, O, *Inner Asian Frontiers of China,* (Boston, 1967).

Levi, Werner, *Modern China's Foreign Policy* (Minneapolis: University of Minnesota Press, 1953).

Lewis, C.G., *Tibetan Venture* (New York : A. S. Barnes, 1968).

Macaulay C., *Report of a Mission to Sikkim and the Tibetan Frontier 1884*. (Kathmandu, 1977).

Maxwell, N., *India's China War*, (Bombay: Jaico, 1971).

Mehra, Parshottam, *The Young Husband Expedition* (New York: Asia Publishing House, 1968).

Mehrotra L.L, *India's Tibet Policy* (New Delhi : TPPRC, Nov. 2000).

Menon, K.N., *Chinese Betrayal of India* (New Delhi : Hind Gyan Mala n.a.)

Murphy, Dervla, *Tibetan Foothold*, (London : John Murray, 1966).

Neterowicz Eva, M., *The Tragedy of Tibet, Journal of Social, Political and Economic Studies, Monograph Series, Volume 19*, (Washington DC : CSES, 1989).

Norbu, Dawa, *Red Star over Tibet* (New Delhi : Sterling Publishers Ltd., 1987).

Norbu, Dawa, *Tibet : The Road Ahead*, (New Delhi : Harper Collins, 1997).

Nowak, M.M., *Liminal "Self", ambigious "Power", The genesis of the 'Rangzen ' metaphor among Tibetan Youth in India*, (Michigan : UMI, 1984).

Official Tibetan and Chinese Positions on the Issue of Tibet Comments on a Xinhua interview on Tibet (Dharamsala : DIIR LTA, 1994).

Palakshappa T.C. *"Tibetans in India : A Case Study of the Mundgod Tibetans"* (New Delhi : Sterling Pub. Pvt. Ltd., 1978).

Patel, Srisha, *Tibetan Refugees in Orissa : An Anthropogentic Study* (Calcutta : Punthi Pustak, 1980).

Patterson, George, N., *Tibet in Revolt* (London : Faber and Faber, 1960).

Powell, Andrew, *Heirs to Tibet : Travel among the exiles in India* (London : Heinemann, 1992).

Rabgay-Ling, *Tibetan Settlement* (Mysore : Office of the Representative)

Racial Discrimination in Tibet (Dharamsala : TCHRD, 2000).

Rahul Ram, *The Government and Politics of Tibet* (New Delhi: Vikas Pub. 1969)

Refugees by Numbers 2000 Edition, (Geneva: UNHCR Publication, 2000),

Richardson, H.E., *Tibet and Its History* (London : OUP 1962).

Samphel, (ed.), *Tibet–84: 25 Years of Struggle and Reconstruction.* (New Delhi : Organizing Committee, Tibet 84, 1984).

Second International conference of Tibet Support Groups Germany June 1996 (Germany : Friedrich Naumann Foundation, 1996).

Sen Chankya, (ed.), *Tibet Disappears (Bombay : Asia Publishing House, 1960).*

Shakya, Tsering, *The Dragon in the Land of Snows : A History of Modern Tibet Since 1947* (London : Pimlico, 1999).

Sharan Shankar (ed.), *India Tibet & China: An Agonizing Reappraisal* (New Delhi : TPPRC, 1996).

Sharma, Swarn Lata, *Tibet : Self-determination in Politics among nations* (New Delhi ; Criterian Pub. 1988).

Shiromany, A.A. (ed.), The Spirit of Tibet : Vision for Human Liberation, Selected speeches and writings of H.H. The XIV Dalai Lama (New Delhi : TPPRC & Vikas, 1995).

Shiromany, A.A. (ed.), *The Political Philosophy of H.H. the XIV Dalai Lama : Selected speeches and writings*, (New Delhi : TPPRC, 1998).

Sinha, A.N., *Law of Citizenship and Aliens in India*, (Bombay : Asia Publishing House, 1962)

Storm, Alex Kristian, *The Quest for grace : Identification and Cultural continuity among Tibetan Refugees in India* (University of Oslo : Institute of Social Anthropology, 1989).

Subba, Tanka B., *Flight and Adaptation : Tibetan Refugees in the Darjeeling – Sikkim Himalaya*, (Dharamsala : Library of Tibetan Works and Archives, 1990).

Tabori, Paul, *The anatomy of exile : A Semantic and Historical Study* (London : Harrap, 1972).

Tales of Terror : Torture in Tibet (Dharamsala : TCHRD, 1999).

The Case Concerning Tibet : Tibet's Sovereignty and the Tibetan People's Right to Self-Determination (New Delhi : TPPRC, 2000).

The Legal Status of Tibet: Three Studies by Leading Jurists (Dharamsala : OIIR, 1989).

Tibetan's in Exile (Dharamsala : Planning Council CTRC, N.A.).

Tibet The Facts: A Report Prepared for UNCHR (Dharamsala: Tibetan Young Buddhist Association, 1990).

Tibet: Proving Truth from Facts (Dharamsala : DIIR, 1996).

Tibet: Human Rights and the Rule of Law. (Switzerland : ICJ December, 1997).

Tibetan Life in Exile: An Information Brochure: (Dharamsala : Council for Home Affairs, 1987).

Tieh – Tseng Li, *The Historical Status of Tibet* (New York: Columbia University King's Crown Press, 1956).

Tsundue, Tenzin, *Crossing the Border* (Mumbai : July 1999).

Turners, An Account of an Embassy to the Court of the Teshoo Lama in Tibet (New Delhi ; 1971 Reprint).

Ugen Gombo, *Tibetan Refugees in Khatmandu Valley : A study in socio-cultural change and continuity and the adaptation of a population in exile.* (University of New York : UMI, 1988).

Warikoo, K, and Norbu Dawa, *Ethnicity and Politics in Central Asia* (New Delhi : South Asian Publishers Pvt. Ltd., 1992).

Articles from Journals and Periodicals

Arpi, Claude, *The Last Rites for Tibet:. Towards Peaceful Co-existence – ? I, Tibetan Review*, March 2002, pp.17 – 21.

Arpi, Claude *The Last Rites For Tibet: Towards Peaceful Co-existence - ? II, Tibetan Review*, April, 2002, pp.19 – 24.

Berreman, Gerald D., *Peoples and Cultures of the Himalayas, Asian Survey* Vol. III. No.6, June 1963, pp.289 – 304.

Bougler, S.C., *China via Tibet, Journal of the Royal Asiatic Society* (N.S.) Vol. X, 1978 (London).

Chakraborty, Nikhil, *India Must Take Initiative, Mainstream*, (New Delhi), 7 October 1995.

Conway, John, S. *Canadian contribution to rehabilitation of Tibetan Refugees, Tibetan Review* (Dharamsala) 13(4), April, 1978, pp.16–17.

Dalai Lama *The International Status of Tibet, India Quarterly* (New Delhi) Vol.XV, No.3, July – September 1959, pp.215–220.

Dalai Lama of Tibet, *Tibet's Case for Self-determination*, Strategic Digest (New Delhi) Vol.XXI, No.5, May 1991 pp.957 – 62.

Dalai Lama, *Its time to prepare New Leaders*, An interview with *Time Magazine* 156(2), 17 July 2000, pp.22–23.

Datta, K. and Chakraborty R, *Freedom in Exile : The Tibetan Refugees of India in Pursuit of rights and identity*, Roy S.K., (ed.), *Refugees and Human Rights*, (New Delhi : Rawat, 2001).

Devoe, Dorsh Marie, *The Refugee Problem and Tibetan Refugees, The Tibet Journal* 6 (3) Autumn, 1981, pp. 22–42.

Dixit, J.N. *Beijing's Asian Aspirations, Outlook* (New Delhi) 25 September 1996.

Doig Desmond, *Bhutan: Mountain Kingdom Between Tibet and India, National Geographic* (Washington D.C.) Vol. 120, September 1961, pp. 384–415.

Dutt Srikant, *Propagand Where India and China Meet, China Report* (New Delhi) Vol. 16, Nos. 5–6, May–June 1980.

Dutta Ray, Sunanda K., *McMahon Line, Tibet and India*, in *Tibet and Peace in South Asia Proceedings of an International Convention, New Delhi*, 12–14, August 1989.

Field A.R., *Bhutan, Kham and The Upper Assam Line, Orbis* (Philadelphia) Summer 1959, Vol. III. No.2 pp.180–192.

Garratt, Kevin, *Tibetan Refugees, asylum seekers, returnees and the refugees convention – predicaments, problems and prospects, The Tibet Journal*, 22(3), Autumn 1997, pp. 18–56.

Ginsburgs George and Mathos Michael *"Tibet's Administration in the Transition Period, - 1951–1954"*, Pacific Affairs (Canada) Vol. XXXII. No.II, June 1959 pp.162–177.

Ginsburgs Georg and Mathos Michael, *Tibet's Administration during the Interregnum, 1954–1959, Pacific Affairs,* Vol. XXXii, No. III September 1959, pp.249–267.

Goldstein, Melvyn, *Tibetan refugees in South India : A new face to the Indo-Tibetan interface. The Tibetan Society Bulletin,* Vol. 9 1975, pp.12–59.

Grunfeld, Tom, *Mao Zedong and Nikita S. Khrushchev exchange views on Tibet, October, 19,. Tibetan Review,* May 2002. pp. 21–22.

Gupta, Indrajit, *Autonomy would be the best solution for Tibet, Tibetan Review,* 32 (8), August 1997, pp. 14–16.

Human Rights in Tibet : A Look at year 2001, Tibetan Bulletin, 6(1), January, April, 2002. pp. 11–13.

India's Assistance to the Tibetan Refugees Since 1959, Tibetan Bulletin, 13(2), March – April, 1982, pp. 15–17.

Jain Girilal, *India's Failure in Tibet,* Sharan Shankar, (ed.), *India Tibet and China : An Agonising Reappraisa,* (New Delhi : Indo-Tibet Friendship Society, 1996) pp. 1–9.

Jethmalani, Ram, *India's Ineffective Diplomacy, Indian Express* (New Delhi), 1994.

Karmapa, Lama, *I wonder if I should not have escaped,* An Interview with *The Week* (Kochi) 19 (22) May 13, 2001. pp. 12–13.

Levi Werner, *India's Himalayan Border, The Contemporary Review,* (London) July 1955, pp. 40–44.

Liu, Melinda, *Tibe: China's Balkan Crisis, Newsweek,* (New York), April, 19, 1999. pp. 34–36.

Liu, Melinda, *When Heaven Shed Blood, Newsweek,* April, 19, 1999. pp. 36–39.

Michael Franz, *A nation in exile : Building an alternative Tibet, Tibetan Review* 21 (6) June 1986. pp. 9–12, 26.

Misra Amalendu, *Tibet in the West and West in Tibet, IASS Newsletter,* Summer 1998 No.16.

Misra, R.C. *Tibetans in Bhutan : Problems of Repatriation, China Report,* Vol. 16, Nos. 9 – 10 September – October. 1982. pp. 25–32.

Mondal Sekh Rahim, *Tibetan Muslim Refugees in India : The Problem and Prospect*, Roy S.K., (ed.), *Refugees and Human Rights*, (New Delhi: Rawat, 2001) pp.236-255.

Mullik B.N. *India Tibet and China, Tibet 84, 25 years of Struggle and Construction* (Organising Committee, Tibet 84, 1984).

Narayan Jayaprakash, *What needs to be done for Tibet, India Quarterly*, Vol. XV, No.3, July–September 1959, pp. 221–228.

Ngawang Dorjee, *Education of Tibetans in India: Treating unequals as equals*, Tibetan Review, 21(5), May 1986, pp. 12–13, 21.

Norbu, Dawa, *Tibetan Refugees and Tibetan Culture, Tibetan Review*, 13(4), April, 1978, pp. 15–16.

-------------------------, *Strategic Development in Tibet, Asian Survey* Vol. XIX No.3, March 1979, pp. 245–257.

-------------------------, *Chinese Strategic Thinking on Tibet and the Himalayan Region, Strategic Analysis*,. Vol.12, no.4, July 1988, pp. 371–395.

-------------------------, *Imperialism and Inner Asia : How British India and Imperial China Redefined the Status of Tibet, [1775 – 1907], Paper presented at Seminar in JNU*, February 16 & 17, 1990.

-------------------------, *China's Dialogue with the Dalai Lama 1978–90 : Pre-negotiation Stage or dead end? Strategic Digest* Vol.XXII No.2 February 1992, pp. 168–182.

-------------------------, *Han Hegemony and Tibetan Ethnicity, International Studies*, 32(3) July–September 1995, pp. 297–314.

-------------------------, *Tibetan Refugees in South Asia : A Case of Peaceful Adjustment*, Muni and Baral, (ed.), *Refugees and Regional Security in South Asia*, (New Delhi : Konark, 1996) pp. 78–98.

-------------------------, *Human Rights as Reflected in UN Resolutions, South East Asia Human Rights NGO on Tibit, TCHRD*, (Dharamsala), 1998, pp. 32–35.

-------------------------, *Refugees from Tibet : Structural Causes of Successful Settlements*, Roy, S.K. (ed.), *Refugee and Human Rights*, (New Delhi : Rawat, 2001) pp. 191–235.

North-East Frontier of India, Notes and Memoranda in *India Quarterly*, Vol XV No.4 October, December 1959, pp. 392–395.

Nothing less than full independence, Tibetan Review, March 2002, pp.22.

Nowak, Margaret, *Change and differentiation in Tibetan Sex roles: The new adult generation in India, Tibetan Review*, 20 (2), February 1985. pp. 10–14.

Nowak, Margaret, (A Book-Review) *Tibetan Refugees: Youth and the new generation of meaning, The Tibet Journal*, 10 (1), Spring 1985, pp.56–58.

Observer, *The Dalai and the Panchen' Tibet's Supreme Incarnate Lamas, India Quarterly*, Vol. XV No.3. July–September 1959, pp.262–289.

Pant Appa, *Indo – Tibetan Relationship – Perspectives and Potential, Tibet 84, 25 Years of Struggle and Construction*. (Organising Comm; Hee, Tibet 84, 1984).

Pande, Pimmi, *Guns over Faith Tibetan Review*, January 2002, pp. 19–22.

Parnov Eremei, *Tibetan Refugees as seen by a Russian, Tibetan Review*, 12 (2 7 3), February, March, 1977, pp. 15–18.

Patterson George N. *Recent Chinese Policies in Tibet and towards the Himalayan Border States, The China Quarterly* (London) No.12, October – December 1962, pp. 191–206.

Pringsheim, Klaus H., *China and India and their Himalayan Border (1961 – 63), Asian Survey*, Vol. III, No.10, October 1963, pp. 474–495.

Rabgay P.T., *Political Games and 4000 Tibetan refugees, Tibetan Bulletin*, 11 (3), August–September 1979, pp. 28–31.

Rinpoche Samdong, *Cultural and Religious Ties Between India and Tibet, Tibet 84, 25 years of Struggle and Construction*. (Organising Committee, Tibet 84, 1984).

Rinpoche Tai Situ, *We'll go when Dalai Lama goes, An Interview with The Week* 19 (22), May 13, 2001. p. 14.

Rose Leo E., *Sino-Indian Rivalary and the Himalayan Border States, Orbis* Vol. 5, No.2, Summer 1961, pp.198–215.

Rose Leo E., *The Himalayan Border States : Buffers in Transition, Asian Survey*, 3. February 1963, pp.116–121.

Sadhu J.N., *Tibetan Refugees in H P acquiring property, Indian Express*, September 15, 1983.

Saklani Girija, *Tibetan Refugees in India : A Sociological Study of an uprooted community, The Tibet Journal*, 3 (4), Winter 1978, pp. 41–46.

Samphel, *Education of Tibetans in India : Mirage of an ideal mixture, Tibetan Review*, 21 (4), April, 1986, pp. 16–17.

Samphel, Thubten, *A Culture in Exile : Tibetan refugees in India, China Report*, 24 (3), July–September 1988, pp. 237–242.

Sampel, Thubten, *Tibetans in New York : Life between two cultures, Tibetan Review*, 24 (12), December 1989, pp. 9–13.

Sarkar Subhash Chandra, *Indian Reactions to Developments in Tibet, India Quarterly* Vol. XV, No.3, July–September 1959, pp.229 – 261.

Schrader, Heiko, *Linked with the World Market – The Case of Tibetan Refugees Community in Nepal, Kailash*, 16 (3 – 4), 1990, pp.187–209.

S.C.S. *Indian Reactions to the Crisis in Tibet, The World Today* (London), Vol.15, No.6, June 1959, pp. 236–246.

Sen, Indra, *Peking Woos Tibetan Refugees, Tibetan Review*, 10 (1), January 1975, p.19.

Shakya Tsering, *Solving the Tibetan Problem, Time*, 15692), 17 July 2002, P. 25.

Sharan, Shankar, *India's Tibet – China Policy, The Hindustan Times* (New Delhi) 16 May, 1996.

Sheikh, Abdul, Ghani, *Tibetan Muslims, The Tibet Journal*, 16(4) winter 1991, pp.86–89.

Shrimali, K.L., *Modern Education and Tibetan Refugee, Tibet 84, 25 years of Struggle and Construction*, (Organising Committee Tibet 84, 1984).

Siddiqui, Ataullah, *Muslims of Tibet, The Tibet Journal*,16 (4), winter1991,pp.71-85.

Smith Warren, *The Transformation of Tibetan National Identity*, Tibetan Review, February 2002, pp. 21 25.

Sondhi, M.L., *Tibet and Indian National Security, Tibet 84, 25 years of Struggle and Construction* (Organising Committee Tibet 84, 1984).

Stobdan P., *Tibet and the Himalayas : A Strategic Dimension to India's Security, Strategic Analysis* – Vol. XIV, No.6 September 1991 pp. 687–702.

Stoddard Heather, *The Lhasa Valley and Tibetan Architecture, IASS Newsletter* (Amsterdam) No.16 Summer 1998. p.11.

Subba Tanka B. *Tibetans in Exile : Economic pursuits and ethnicity* Paper presented at JNU Seminar *Ethnicity, Politics & Development in Central Asia,* February 16 & 17, 1990.

Thinley Choephel, *Tibetan refugees visiting occupied Tibet, Rangzen,* 11 (3), July–September 1986, pp. 22–24.

Tibetan Muslim refugees in Kashmir, Tibetan Review, 11(5), May 1976, pp.15–17.

Tibetan Refugees in Ladakh Tibetan Review, 8-9, August-September,1969 pp.12-13.

Tibet : Rethinking the Riddle, Time (Hongkong) 156(2) July 17, 2000 pp. 18–24.

Van Walt Van Praag, (Michael C.) *Population Transfer and the Survival of the Tibetan Identity, Strategic Digest,* January 1988.

Vohra Sahadev, *The North–Eastern Frontier of India and China's Claim Strategic Analysis.* Vol.XII No.IX. December, 1989 pp. 931–948.

William, Peters, *Unresolved Problem of Tibet, Asian Affairs,* June 1998.

Yang Yun – Yuan, *Controversies Over Tibet: China Verses India, 1947–1949, The China Quarterly* (III) September 1987.

INDEX

❑❑❑